Affiliating with Over the Hill Gang International as members, and then ultimately running it for 15 years, became a treasure! Not only did we continue enjoying a sport we loved with like-minded people, but we found so many unexpected pleasures. Not only did we bring hundreds of people together to become lifelong friends, but we became part of that lifelong chain of friendship. We did all this while enjoying the beautiful mountains around the world. The stories and lessons in this book about the magic of senior skiing make this a fascinating read.

Sherrie & Dennis Beasley, Owners of Over the Hill Gang International, 1991-2006

● ● ●

The history presented in *Peak Performers* is a testament to the joy alpine skiing brings to many late into their lives and the strong dedication of individuals associated with the Over The Hill Gang. The joy and passion expressed throughout this book makes it a must read for all who embrace the love for alpine adventure.

Ryan Hellman, President, Hellman & Associates, Inc., Environmental Health & Safety Compliance Advisers

● ● ●

Peak Performers is a great tribute to the Pioneers who put their lives on the line to keep our country safe during World War II and to the same pioneers who helped build the foundation that made the sport of skiing in the United States what it is today. It is also a tribute to those same pioneers, and many others, who have worked over the years to keep family and friends involved in our sport, both physically and socially, as they age. Congratulations to the authors and the wonderful people featured in this book.

Gary DeFrange, Retired President, Winter Park Resort

From the very beginning of my role as Copper Mountain Resort's CEO, I have been an advocate of the concept of the Over the Hill Gang (OHG). For years we saw the evolution of the ski industry that was started and energized by the returning veterans of the 10th Mountain Division from WWII. Those visionaries saw skiing not only as a strategic tool of the war but, as a sport with lifetime benefits for all who participated.

The OHG reflected the enthusiasm of those original visionaries and added not only the benefits of enjoying a winter sport but the comradery of skiing with someone in your sphere of life experiences. They expanded their program to include a social atmosphere outside of the skiing that bound them together in life-long friendships.

None of this would have been possible without the vision of the three founders, Bill Magill, Tom Stein, and Moe Mosley. They were the ones who saw the demand, structured the program and recognized the benefits beyond just the skiing experience. Their leadership and enthusiasm for the OHG was transferred to the staff, the resort and the membership of the OHG. In addition, there was a tremendous commitment by the Guides who became an integral part of the program. They took on the challenges of implementing a ski program to all levels of participants. They were enthusiastic and became advocates of the OHG beyond the expectations of everyone involved.

I congratulate Moe Mosley on his commitment to the OHG and his perseverance in publishing this wonderful history of a program that so many of us were fortunate to be a part of.

Harry Mosgrove, former CEO of Copper Mountain

* * *

The story of the Over the Hill Gang is so inspiring. If you like good stories *Peak Performers* is full of them. Personally, I love storytelling and thoroughly appreciate hearing these.

OHG has touched many lives in many ways. In my over 4 decades of working with Copper Ski and Ride School, there is not one program that has had a broader continuous positive impact. Tom Stein, Bill Magill and Moe Mosley's brilliantly simple idea to develop a senior skiing program became our country's best. Through a little luck, a lot of love and labor, OHG found its feet and hit the slopes. The success and vast acceptance of OHG spread across Colorado, the U.S and went International. Often imitated but never duplicated, Copper Mountain's Over the Hill Gang is recognized as the best senior skiing program in our industry. It truly has an enviable reputation.

Fate combined to bring together a fearless trio, Professor Tom, Father Bill and Coach Moe. Watching their forming process was amazing. They were a perfect team. We sometimes called them The Brain, The Bible and The Body. Moe, of course, was The Body. Moe is one strong skier and one stubborn workaholic. He never missed an OHG day for lord knows how many years. Moe is one of the most motivating individuals I know. Father Bill married my wife Linda and I and Moe Dixon played at our wedding. OHG is part of our heart. Copper has entered my soul.

This intriguing story centers around an amazing mountain. Copper is a special place. Its beauty is hard to describe. Moe has personally grown my spiritual awareness of how we live with nature and each other. Many stories in his book reflect our common spiritual love that just so happens to center around skiing, the best sport on the planet we share.

So, I take this moment to thank Moe for making this book possible. I learned a lot and laughed even more. If you feel a tear forming, let it flow. Let it go. It may turn left and right down your cheek. Cool!

Don Coleman, Copper Ski and Ride School

* * *

Peak Performers takes you to a pivotal time in skiing's history, during exciting resort development and industry formation. Grounded in the true spirit of human connection, before we started counting likes, swipes and follows, the story of the Over the Hill Gang's foundation, growth and influence will entice you join the fraternity of passionate snow sports enthusiasts regardless of your age. But the real feat of *Peak Performers* is how it documents camaraderie as not only a founding mission for Over the Hill Gang, but as a significant motive for snow sport participation today. It is impossible to read *Peak Performers* and not want to call your ski buddies and meet them on the hill as soon as possible.

Jennifer Rudolph,
Corporate Communications
for POWDR Corp.

PEAK
PERFORMERS

The Remarkable History and Adventures of a Seniors Skiing Program in America

Stephen S. Hultquist and Lance H.K. Secretan

with Moe Mosley

ISBN 978-0-9865654-6-5

Published by the Secretan Center Inc.
Caledon, Ontario, Canada

Cover & text design: Kim Monteforte, WeMakeBooks.ca
Cover photo: Tripp Fay, Copper Mountain Resort

Printed in Canada

Dedication

We dedicate this book and journey to:

- Those earlier year ski pioneers, who, for the love of the sport, and solitude of the mountains that they loved in the United States and abroad, introduced millions to skiing;

- The parties that attended the Copper Mountain OHG Charter Membership Meeting on April 19, 1978;

- The Charter Members, former, present, deceased, and to all future members of their senior ski organization;

- The former, present, and deceased guides, the future PSIA members who become OHG guides, the ski patrol, instructors, management, and employees of the mountains we ski and the employees of all senior ski organizations:

  - The 10th Mountain Division

  - Over the Hill Gang Ski Team, Inc. (OHG, Copper Mountain, Colorado)

  - SkiMeisters (Winter Park, Colorado)

  - Over the Hill Gang International, Inc. (OHGI, multiple ski areas)

    - Loose Goose Group International
    - A-Basin
    - Loveland

- Ski Cooper
- Snowmass
- Steamboat
- Winter Park
- Monarch
- Powderhorn (Young at Heart)
- Breckenridge (Vail Resorts)
- Keystone (Vail Resorts)
- Vail (Vail Resorts)

- PSIA—Professional Ski Instructors Association/ Rocky Mountain Division
- PSIA—Professional Ski Instructors Association/ National
- NSAA—National Ski Areas Association (Representing 313+ ski areas)

Table of Contents

Introduction

It was October 2nd, 2015 in Vail, an amazing Colorado fall day with a crystal clear sky and the air just hinting at the promise of snow for the upcoming El Niño season. The town was making ready for the annual Colorado Ski and Snowboard Museum Hall of Fame gala, preparing for the six new inductees who would be added to the 207 previous Hall of Fame members with more than 600 guests attending.

There were also six Annual Recognition Awards, including the Top of the Hill Award, recognizing an institution or entity that has contributed to the development of skiing in Colorado.

The 2015 award winner was Jerry "Moe" Mosley and the Copper Mountain Over the Hill Gang. Moe accepted the award on behalf of the three original founders, and on November 4th, Moe presented the award to the Copper Mountain management team, reinforcing the founders' mantra that the program relied on three interconnected components, starting with the mountain. Although Moe insisted that the award was for the mountain and the program, it was clear from reading the nominations that

Moe was the award's inspiration. His vision, commitment, and humble service to the program from its inception until his retirement in 2012 (having never missed a scheduled day at the Copper Ski School over nearly 40 years!) were the primary factors in its success.

The Over the Hill Gang influenced and changed skiing in Colorado and worldwide. It continues to promote physical and mental health of members aged 50 and over by providing skiing, social, and fraternal activities. It is a unique program that created a context for senior skiing worldwide.

The Economist Magazine reported in its January 25, 2014 issue, "The Over the Hill Gang does not sound menacing. But the members of this Colorado-based skiing group for the over-50's and their peers now dominate the slopes. Baby boomers have propped up America's ski resorts for longer than anyone expected. The average age of customers rose from 33 years old in 1997-98 to 39 years old in the 2013 season, according to the National Ski Areas Association, and the share over 55 has risen from 7% to 17%. "Grays on trays" (as one snowboarding outfit calls them) ski more than youngsters, since they have more free time and money."

Every season, the hundreds of members of the Copper Mountain Over the Hill Gang take over the base area 4 mornings a week, Saturday, Sunday, Tuesday, and Wednesday. Together, they'll ski millions of vertical feet, hundreds of runs, take dozens of special all-day clinics to learn more about skiing competently in different conditions and terrain, improving their skills every day, every year—together. Over the years, members have gone from first time skiers and those who visit the mountains for a few days a year, to advanced skiers. They are members of the alpine community who ski almost every day, continue to improve, and enjoy every turn as they eagerly look forward to the next.

It all started in 1976 when a trio of part-time PSIA ski instructors at the young Copper Mountain Resort in Colorado came up with an idea for a ski program for adults who were 45 and over to enjoy the mountains, each other, and the sport of alpine skiing that had been such a passion for them and others.

This program, to be named the Over the Hill Gang, became a true force in skiing in Colorado and beyond.

This book is an informal history of this organization and its progeny from then to now.

The book overviews more than 40 years of history from the major contributors to the experienced, senior skier programs of the last four decades in Colorado. The story begins inauspiciously during a season that held little promise...

This book is dedicated to the mountains and all of those who have connected to and through it with the senior skiing programs.

It is our hope that you will find the book interesting and enjoyable. Read it as though you are skiing through decades of deep powder history into a new and positive era of recreation and health for individuals who choose mountains for challenge and enjoyment.

This book is a history of the Copper Mountain Over the Hill Gang and the people who made it so successful. As OHG guide and instructor, Winnie Johnson wrote: "I will always treasure my years as an OHG Guide. By watching the OHG members enjoy their 'senior' years, I believe that I have learned how to grow old with grace and joy. When I first started guiding, as a young 33-year-old, I was in awe of their 'can do' attitude, their excitement in learning new skills, and their inability to allow something as 'simple' as a broken bone or a heart attack to keep them down for long. Now, in my early 70's, I appreciate all they have taught me—far more than I ever taught them."

Winnie was the third guide to join the OHG program after its founding, and after the 2016/2017 season she retired from the Copper Mountain Ski & Ride School after 41 years of service to the guests of Copper Mountain, more than 35 of those she served as a guide in the Over the Hill Gang. Winnie's spirit of joyfully sharing the mountains and the sport continued to inspire the guests through her very last day as a guide. She embodies the very best of the OHG.

Perhaps Don Coleman summed up the essence as he wrote in his nomination letter about Jerry "Moe" Mosley for the Hall of Fame, "The beautiful part of the OHG is its unique experience. It's not about the guides, it's about the members sharing and the guides caring. Members' memories of best runs, greatest days, and the dearness of new, lifelong friends, echo through forty-odd years."

After decades of amazing experiences, the Copper Mountain Over the Hill Gang program is still going strong with 52-plus guided ski days each season. For more information about the current programs, contact Copper Mountain by email at *OHG@coppercolorado.com* or call Copper Mountain Ski & Ride School at +1-970-968-3089.

THE FOUNDERS OF OHG

They have often been called the "Three Working Founders", and they worked so closely together that they seemed to be a committee of one.

(left to right) **Jerry "Moe" Mosley**—Born in Canton, Ohio, moved to Colorado after the Korean Conflict. He graduated from The University of Northern Colorado. He has been the owner of a Federal Compliance Consulting Firm and still skis with an OHG group. Moe has been a member of the Rocky Mountain PSIA/AASI since 1973. **Bill Magill**—Known by many as the Reverend William Hazer "Father Bill" Magill, PhD—Born in Oklahoma, raised in Texas, educated at Texas A&M and Nashotah House Seminary. Bill served as a Marine Corps Fighter Pilot in WWII. He received two Distinguished Flying Crosses, five Air Medals and flew 89 missions. Father Bill Magill was a Master Mason and a Shriner, and was a member of the Home Building Construction Industry for a short time. We lost Father Bill on 1/26/2011. **Tom Stein**—Born in Chicago, Illinois, an alumnus of Carleton College, moved to Colorado and first taught skiing at Winter Park and Keystone. He then moved to Copper during the 1974/75 season. Tom's full-time occupation was Director of Communications for the University of Colorado, and he also served on the Colorado Governor's Fitness Committee. We lost Tom on 2/21/07.

—Stephen S. Hultquist and Lance H.K. Secretan with Moe Mosley

The Genesis of Skiing in the United States

Prior to WWII, winter sports in the United States were limited to very small, isolated groups spread throughout snowy and alpine areas of the country. Only a very small percentage of individuals participated in any winter sports.

The burgeoning winter sports world in the U.S. today is a credit to the work of a few die-hard skiers who developed their passion for the sport during their training for service in WWII. Before embarking on an overview of senior skiing in Colorado and the Copper Mountain Over the Hill Gang, it's important to offer a tribute to those members of the famous 10th Mountain Division (Light Infantry) and the mountain troops of other nations that fought with valor in that great conflict. After the war, these men joined forces and became great friends, developers, and leaders in the earliest days of the nascent ski industry, and to this day they have continued to work tirelessly on the development of skiing in the United States.

After having trained in the Rocky Mountains, many of the returning troops came back to live in the high country of Colorado. Those veterans have served in every aspect of the sport of skiing, including mountain operations, resort development and planning, teaching, patrolling the slopes, and coaching young racers and other competitors.

Of all the ski areas in Colorado, few did not benefit from their expertise, vision, and insights. They shaped new ski areas and provided their innovative improvements that laid the foundation for the Colorado ski industry and the wider ski industry across the United States.

This tribute is to those early ski pioneers and all the senior ski programs including participants, mountains, patrol, instructors, guides, and our fellow 10th Mountain Division brothers. Among the early 10th Mountain Division members were:

Earl Clark:
>   Colorado Ski Hall of Fame inductee
>   President of the National Association of the 10th Mountain Division for seven years
>   Vermont Ski Hall of Fame inductee
>   President, then Board Member of Over the Hill Gang, International, Inc.
>   And recipient of many additional awards and honors

Dick Over:
>   Member of the 10th Mountain Division

Member of the Over the Hill Gang Ski Team
   of Copper Mountain Colorado
Pennsylvania Ski Hall of Fame inductee
Member of SkiMeisters of Winter Park, Colorado
And recipient of many additional awards
   and honors

Additional information, including full accounts of the 10th Mountain Division history, unit and individual combat action, may be found in the Regimental and integral unit component histories, articles, photographs, books and films, at the Division's Resource Center at the Denver Public Library, Western History Department, *www.denver library.org* and at the Colorado Historical Society, *www.coloradohistory.org*, as well as at the National Association of the 10th Mountain Division website, *www.10thmtndiv assoc.org* and *https://en.wikipedia.org/wiki/10th_Mountain_Division_(United_States)*.

THE DEVELOPMENT OF CAMP HALE

On December 7, 1941, bombs dropped on Pearl Harbor and America entered WWII. The US military decided to expand the concept of mountain warfare troops. They needed to find an appropriately large area to house the expected three regiments of 1,000 troops each which would make up a full division.

They chose an area located in Pando Valley, Colorado between Leadville and what is now Vail. A railway ran directly through the valley, providing easy accessibility. This valley became Camp Hale.

The camp was named for Brigadier General Irving Hale of Denver, a West Point graduate, veteran of the Spanish American War, and one of the founders of the Veterans of Foreign Wars.

The camp was built with typical wartime zeal. Beginning on April 10, 1942, a veritable army of workmen, drawn by the lure of an hourly wage of $1.10, put up their own transient work camp. They covered the swamp-flat with 2 million cubic yards of earth excavated from the surrounding hillsides, chopped down seventeen square miles of willows, straightened the twisty Eagle River, rerouted and rebuilt a highway, laid railroad track, and constructed a complete army camp by early December, 1942—all in the amazingly short time of 8 months!

The nearby mining town of Leadville experienced a boom it hadn't seen since most of the gold and silver mines shut down in the late 1800s, and it saw its population swell from 1,800 in June of 1942 to almost 10,000 by August of that year.

Under the brilliant blue Colorado sky, Camp Hale gleamed like a pearl. The desolate valley was filled with more than eight hundred white painted buildings, barracks, mule barns, blacksmith shops, chapels, mess halls, post exchanges, a hospital, service clubs, day rooms, a field house, an officer's club, theaters, motor pools, a supply depot, warehouses, a stockade, a post office, and even a mortuary (at least twenty-eight soldiers died at Hale due to illness, injury, training mishaps, auto accidents, and a plane crash). All this provided accommodations for 16,392 officers and enlisted men together with 3,925 horses and mules. In addition, there was a ski slope, rifle range, bayonet drill field, grenade court, artillery range, and combat village—all built in eight months!

In July, 1943, the 87th Regiment was developed into the evolving 10th Mountain Division. After returning from 6 months tour of duty at Kiska Island, Alaska, the 86th Regiment was formed. Part of the original 87th also became the new 85th Regiment which, in turn, became part of the 10th Mountain Division. The 10th Mountain Division was thus made up of the 85th, 86th, and 87th Regiments.

This is where our early ski pioneers received their ski education and training.

The US Army's Tenth Mountain Division was an elite group of 17,000 who served during WWII as ski troopers and defeated the Germans in the battle of Riva Ridge in Italy. They were activated in 1941 and spent four years of training at Camp Hale near Leadville where they learned artillery, rock climbing, brutally cold winter survival and many other skills. Inspired by the ski troops of Finland that defeated the Russians, Charles "Minnie" Dole appealed to the US Army to establish this corps. Expert skiers from the Northeast and other parts of the US joined, as well as non-skiing Midwesterners drafted to handle the pack animals. Their skis were made of wood and over seven feet long. The troops wore wool, leather, and carried 93 pound packs.

Casualties were heavy among the corps with 987 killed in combat and around 4,000 injured. Many members of the Tenth that returned came back to a life in the ski industry. Minnie Dole had already established the National Ski Patrol. John Litchfield developed Aspen, while Pete Seibert established Vail, and Ernie Blake founded Taos.

Former Vice President Bob Dole was a member of the Tenth Mountain Division.

There is a memorial near Ski Cooper to the troops who gave their lives, providing an opportunity to reflect on the incredible effort and cost. The Tenth Mountain Division is still active and is based at Fort Drum in New York. (Source: Tom Brokaw's video "Triumph of the Tenth" and Richard "Dick" Over, former member of the Tenth Mountain Division Signal Corps).

The Short History of the Area Now Called Copper Mountain

The valley east of Vail Pass once was a rich hunting ground for the Ute and Arapahoe Native American Tribes and Nations. They would often summer in and around the valley before migrating back to warmer areas of the region for the winter to avoid the cold and snow. Their high country summer home would eventually create a mecca for those who found so much joy and recreation in the majesty and power of the mountains.

During the western expansion of the United States, and the gold and silver booms in Colorado, the area was called Wheeler Junction or Wheeler Flats, after Judge John S. Wheeler who lived in this area during the flurry of mining and lumbering activity in the latter part of the 19th century. Like many of Colorado's mountain towns, this area was abandoned by the turn of the century with

US Forest Service records showing that the town was completely abandoned in 1907. Wheeler Flats faded into oblivion by the very early part of the century, following the departure of its namesake and his family.

In 1940, the Custer and Beeler families took possession of the west end of the old Wheeler property and, in 1941, they established a small mining operation.

In the late 1940's, Willy Schaeffler, former head of the U.S. Ski Team, was one of the first to recognize the potential of the mountain as a ski area. Willy scouted Copper Mountain from Union Peak to Spaulding Bowl, determining it was a natural fit for a ski area. He offered to buy the land from the Forest Service, but was blocked by the then-steep price tag of $30.00 per acre.

In 1954, the District Forest Ranger, Paul Hauk, also saw Copper as a great skiing mountain, stating in a report that "it amazed him that no one had done anything with it" as of that date. Over the years, developers continued to eye Copper Mountain as a ski area, but it remained a gem yet to be polished.

Then, 15 years later, the obvious potential began to inspire progress. One crucial step towards realizing Copper Mountain as a ski area was the publication of a Forest Service Report in 1969 stating, "If there ever was a mountain that had the terrain great for skiing, it would be Copper Mountain. ... It is probably the most outstanding potential ski area available in the Arapahoe National Forest and possibly in Colorado."

THE BUILDING OF COPPER MOUNTAIN RESORT

After reading the Forest Service Reports about Copper, Chuck Froelicher, who was Headmaster of Colorado Academy Prep School and Director of a mining corporation, asked Chuck Lewis to explore the area. Lewis, then the Executive Vice President and Treasurer at Vail Associates, owners of Vail Ski Resort, took a cross-country ski tour of Copper Mountain and saw what Willy Schaeffler and District Forest Ranger Hauk had seen: a great location for a ski area with varied, naturally-divided terrain, and easy accessibility for guests.

This time, however, the dream didn't die, as Chuck Froelicher, along with 16 other investors, collected $500,000 in capital to form Copper Mountain Associates. Chuck Lewis was named general partner and given the ambitious responsibility of developing the resort from the ground up. With the purchase of 280 acres of base-area land from Eugene Sanders, Copper Mountain Resort was born.

Chuck Lewis logged over 150,000 air miles in an effort to raise the $6 million investment required to begin the first phase of the plan. After all that work, Chuck eventually found the money in his backyard about 600 yards from his office in Denver, when Fulenwider Management & Development Company agreed to terms, and construction began.

On August 12, 1969, a study permit was issued by the Forest Service for approximately 2,500 acres of future ski trails in the Arapahoe National Forest for what would become Copper Mountain Resort.

Thus, Copper Mountain was born of a master plan, unique at the time in both depth and detail. Prior to the beginning of construction in 1971, the developers spent more than two years studying every aspect of the project, including financing a great number of area studies critical to creating a unique recreation resort.

An additional two years of construction would follow before the resort opened.

One of the hallmarks of Copper's development was the "can do" attitude exhibited by Chuck Lewis and his team. For example, when timber from trail cutting became difficult to discard, they came up with the entrepreneurial idea of forming the Thick & Thin Lumber Co. to sell it.

Similar entrepreneurial prowess was evident when concrete to anchor lift towers proved too pricey to purchase from outside sources, and so the Pretty Lumpy Concrete Co. came into being. Gravel was mined on-site, as well, forming several lakes now seen at the base area and around the golf course.

And then there's the story of the beavers.

The valley was home to a family of beavers who dammed the creek and lived off the area near where the Copper Mountain Club Med building was built, which has since become The EDGE employee housing and cafeteria, after being featured in the movie Copper Mountain starring the young Jim Carrey.

Development was moving forward, but the large beaver population and their dams turned Copper into a tangle of willow marshes. Negotiations with the beavers began, but as soon as Copper workers moved the dams, the beavers would rebuild them.

Copper tagged the beavers and moved them multiple times, but it became obvious that the ski area and beavers couldn't negotiate a coexistence agreement, so a special mulcher machine from Canada encouraged the beavers to move across the highway and down the canyon. The time and care the Copper team used in their relationship with the beavers demonstrates the respect that the management and the entire team had for the mountain, the valley, and its wildlife, from the very beginning.

THE FIRST SKIERS

In the spring and summer of 1971, Copper's first trails were cut and the mountain opened for snow-cat skiing in November of that year. During this time, Chuck Lewis also instilled in the team the concept that the resort wasn't simply a ski area offering basic uphill and downhill utility, but a services business focused on delivering excellence to guests who came to create their own alpine experience.

During the 20th anniversary celebration of Copper Mountain, a local paper interviewed Chris Colman, who started working at Copper Mountain in the summer of 1971 and, as of this writing, is still at Copper Mountain. He was honored in March 2012 for 40 years of service.

In the interview, Chris explained that the summer of 1972 was a busy one for the Copper crew: "We put in B, C, E, F, and G chairs that summer," he said, "and we also built the Center Building, Solitude Station, cut trails, and installed all the utilities."

At the beginning, chairlifts were labeled with letters and ski runs were numbered until names were selected later.

"There were so many vehicles running up and down the mountain," said Colman, "that they almost needed a traffic cop."

There was an amazing amount of effort necessary to accomplish so much heavy industrial construction over a single summer, especially given the challenges of altitude and the alpine environment with such a short summer.

YEAR BUILT	LIFT NAME
1971/72	B, C, E, F, G
1973	B1 & I
1975	Mitey Mite
1976	H
1977	J
1979	A & C1
1981	K, L, T
1982	R
1983	S
1985	A1 (Resolution) & Storm King
1986	O1/Flyer
1989	O2/Eagle
1994	T-Rex
1995	#6/Mountain Chief
1996	#4/Black Jack
1997	Stinger (began construction)
1998	Super Bee, Excelerator, Glide
1999	Eagle/Flyer bottom terminal relocates
2000	Rug Rat, Easy Rider
2002	Sling Shoot (Tubing handle tow)
2006	Stinger (tubing conveyor completed)

YEAR BUILT	LIFT NAME
2011	Union Creek Quad
2013	Celebrity Ridge
2017	Kokomo Quad

Figure 1: The History of the Construction of Copper Mountain Lifts as of 2017

Many members of the team that built Copper Mountain were intertwined through friends and family relationships with the well-known 10th Mountain Division. For example, Chuck Lewis himself was a member of the Mountain Weather Training Command.

Those beginning years of Copper Mountain's construction and skiing drew the founding group of employees and family members into a very tight and proud community. Even today, they continue to get together periodically to visit and share old stories and reminisce. Some of the early employees in 1971-1972 were:

Some Copper Mountain team members

Chuck Lewis	Paul Jacobs
George Beardsley	Penny Lewis
Dale Bome	Bill Loring
Rita Cavnar	Ron Martin
Chris Colman	Dean Michaels
Andy Daly	Mike Michaels
Jerry Decker	Marcel Mouler
Dean East	Don Peterson
Joe Fedore	Arthur "Buckets" Richburg
Deryl Gingery	Bob Ryan

Robbie Scholl   Susan Smith
Herb Settle   Mike Smith
George Shaw   Kevin Williams
Ken Shultz

There were always many projects going on and many are not documented, but Copper Mountain was Colorado's first Public Utility District (PUD), and Don Peterson's designs for Copper Mountain Water and Sanitation District were some of the first Title 32 Special Districts in Colorado.

SNOWCAT POWDER TOURS

Before the resort opened for lift-served skiing, the resort ran limited-access powder tours by snowcat. There were little more than 2,000 paid customers, but even so, there were some interesting stories from that first year.

For example, the last Cat Powder Tour of the winter season took place just prior to the season closing party. The Denver Copper Mountain Staff wanted to take a snowcat tour just before the party, but the last driver using the cat to deliver guests to the top of the ski runs didn't refuel it at the end of the day. Communication was limited since the season was ending and, unfortunately, the driver taking the Denver ladies on the snowcat tour didn't check the fuel level before he left the base.

As mentioned earlier, the ski runs were labeled with trail numbers, and they ran out of gas at the top of #15 (since renamed Collage). That meant the driver and all of the ladies in their evening dresses and in snowboots walked down below Solitude via trail #25 (since renamed Fair Play) where Chuck Lewis found them.

What a sight it must have been to see those ladies dressed for a party clomping through the powder mid-mountain towards the base. We can only imagine the emotions they must have experienced, and the stories they would tell for the rest of their lives. At the time of the event, however, Mr. Lewis wasn't a happy camper—especially since they had to find a way to retrieve the cat the next day.

With all the changes to the winter sports industry since those halcyon days, Copper Mountain may well be the last ski mountain built out of love. Over the course of time, it became clear that the terrain covered by the mountain would eventually expand to the full extent of their master plan. Many of those early skiers looked forward to the adventure of skiing new untracked snow in areas of the mountain that were previously too danger-ous and difficult to access without the involvement of the Copper Mountain Professional Ski Patrol to provide snowpack analysis and avalanche control.

The developers of mountain ski areas were generally concerned when their expansion programs started and Copper Mountain was no exception. Remember, alpine resorts employ adventurous people who can get carried away exploring new areas of their mountain environment. Many of them want to keep their secret stashes of good snow to themselves, but ultimately, the resort exists for the guests, and the expansion of Copper over the years has been devoted to providing a joyful experience for guests and employees, and will continue to do so in the future.

MOUNTAIN EXPANSION

Chuck Lewis was never a fan of expanding lifts into the more avalanche prone areas of Copper Mountain, since he felt that the expense of controlling and managing the difficult terrain and the small number of people who skied that type of terrain in those early days made such expansion unfeasible. However, he had the foresight to include them in the original US Forest Service permit application, including Union and Spaulding Bowls. After some years, the clientele and capabilities of skiers and snowboarders began to grow and change, so Copper Mountain started an aggressive expansion into those steeper and more natural areas.

Union Bowl was the first to see lift service (1982), then Spaulding Bowl (1985), followed by Copper Bowl (1995). Spaulding was a little trickier than Copper Bowl, though —the lift layout was delicate because of wetlands, the terrain was challenging because of the side hill fall lines, the necessary avalanche control work was extensive, and it also had a southern exposure. These factors meant that the area wasn't ideal for expansion. But on a good snow day, it offers some of the best skiing at Copper Mountain.

The Copper Mountain team began laying out A1 (now known as the Resolution chairlift) in 1983. They started by locating the lift terminal first and then worked the trail layout from there. Copper could do most of the trail layout from existing lift access, which at the time was from the top of the two summit chairs: E and B1. The team were also trying to locate another lift, A2 (which was never built) that would serve the Spaulding Glade terrain to the south of A1. For this they would have to go to the top of Spaulding Bowl via snowcat and ski the run now called Park Place, the furthermost eastern trail of Spaulding Bowl.

It is in this area that Copper Mountain staff had one of the more storied experiences of the early days.

From the beginning, the mountain management staff were very aggressive and confident skiers. One day, five employees decided to take another look at the top terminal of the planned A2 lift. All but one of them were self-proclaimed experts on snow. Two of them had beacons (devices used to locate those buried in an avalanche), but the rest of the group did not, since they weren't planning on skiing anything steep or dangerous. However, the snow conditions that day were marginal, at best. It was spring-time, and the mountain's natural snow surface was a windblown, breakable crust.

To be safe, they avoided all the steep chutes in Spaulding Bowl and skied over to the future site of the top terminal of A2 where the pitch of the terrain was less steep. After a quick inspection, they all skied down the ridge of Park Place to make their way towards better snow conditions. The two patrollers with beacons dropped off to the east side of Park Place to see if the snow was any better. Two others were sure it would be just more breakable crust, so they avoided it. The next thing heard as they were skiing down was one of the two who broke off yelling, "Avalanche! Avalanche! Buried! Buried!" The others could not see the slide because they were on a different aspect of the slope and slightly ahead of them to the west, so they turned around and side-stepped their way back up and to the east where they could finally get a look at what happened.

Park Place has a short little face on the west side 300-400 feet long. What they saw they couldn't believe. There was a five foot deep fracture line where you could see tracks etched into the crust and then disappearing into space where once there was snow. The patroller who had witnessed the whole thing was standing at the top of the fracture line. He yelled that his partner had ridden the slab a couple hundred feet until it crumbled and sucked him under and then stopped moving. He pointed to where he thought his partner was.

As quickly as they could, the group made it to the bottom of the release, then removed their skis and tried to crawl over Volkswagen-sized blocks of snow to where they thought their partner was buried. They were all yelling for him when suddenly his hand, sporting a bird finger, popped out between the blocks of snow.

Because the slide had taken the snow off the mountain all the way to the ground, they had to traverse around the slide area and climb back up to him. They did not have shovels so they carried their skis to use as improvised shovels, digging as they quickly crawled up and over huge blocks of snow that were now turning into the consistency of concrete. They reached their colleague who was trapped between two huge blocks of snow, lying with his head downhill and parallel to the ground with his hand sticking out between the blocks. They proceeded to dig him out with the tails of their skis, while he cussed the entire time. The team had radioed earlier to patrol headquarters to initiate a rescue but they were able to extricate their teammate before the other patrollers arrived. They extracted him in a matter of minutes with everything intact except a pole that he lost during the slide. He was mostly expressing his anger over losing his pole, yet underneath the bluster, he was thankful for their energy and hard work—it saved his life.

After they had each caught their breath and recovered their composure, one of them looked at all the others and said, "Ok, boys. From now on, let's stick together!" They all gave him the thumbs up and took off down the hill where the snow conditions had improved and within seconds they were all skiing their own lines as if nothing had happened, and today you will find skiers still doing the same thing there every day.

At the end of their eventful day, they were unconcerned, behaving as if nothing unusual had happened. Even today, no one knows whether or not the incident was reported to the US Forest Service or to any authority, as required. They had called off the patrol before they deployed. Just like a family, they all conducted an amateur medical diagnosis of the injured member of their party, concluding that he had possible broken ribs and advised him to go home and self-medicate.

Therein lies a good example of why Chuck Lewis never wanted to expand that terrain under his watch: Even the best, most aggressive, confident skiers can get into trouble by not following the most careful and wise choices, being intimately, and constantly, aware of snowpack characteristics, and obeying closures.

These are just some of the things that go into building

a ski area and the source of the grey hair of owners and operators!

EARLY DAYS OF THE SKI RESORT

During the building of Copper Mountain, the team received an environmental award recognizing their sensitive and thoughtful planning that honored the gorgeous environment of the mountain and its surroundings.

On November 30, 1972, Copper Mountain Resort opened to the public with five ski lifts, 14 miles of trails, and six new buildings. Lift tickets started at $7.50 per day and were later increased to $9.00.

During that first year, Jim Isham, the Ski School Director, started to build a quality ski school. When Jim returned to Taos, NM, Butch Graves took over the ski school and, together with Floyd Bashant and the Copper Mountain staff, continued building a talented team of instructors and a high quality, internationally recognized ski school.

The official dedication ceremonies for Copper Mountain Resort were held on February 23, 1973. The dedication ski race was held on run #29. On that trail, Colorado Governor Love broke his leg, so the name of the ski run was later changed to Loverly in his honor.

As mentioned earlier, in those early days, all of the trails were assigned numbers. Of course, some old-timers stuck to using the numbers for many years, long after they were named. So you might hear someone say, "The bumps are good on 19," and you would head over to Brennan's Grin to see. If you heard that the powder was deep on 22, you would head to Hallelujah to enjoy it for yourself. If you heard 16 was groomed and you wanted to ski it, you would head to American Flyer. Even today, some of the numbers remain hidden within the names. For instance, Trail 2 is now called Too Much, Trail 3 is now known as Triple Treat and Trail 4 is now called Formidable. Trail 1 is now called Far East—say it quickly and it might sound like "first". Take a look at the trail map and see if you can find some of them. Here's a hint: one of them is a glade.

All through this time, Copper Mountain continued growing and building a highly regarded resort with an exceptional ski school, ski patrol, and mountain staff.

The Beginning of the OHG

During the 1974-1975 ski season after a day on the Hill, in order to avoid the Denver-bound traffic heading to the Front Range, members of the Ski School would sit around, talk and strategize about ways to increase Copper's business. The Reverend William Magill (now known as "Father Bill" by almost everyone) and some other instructors discussed the age of the skiers they were seeing on the mountain. Father Bill thought the mountain was losing revenue since many of the middle aged skiers gave up the sport after their children grew up and left home.

The early months of the 1975/1976 ski season had limited snow. In fact, to do their training, instructors shoveled snow out of the trees onto run #18 on Copper Mountain (since renamed Copperopolis), where early-season training was held.

During a meeting of the supervisor and instructors,

the ski school Director was looking for methods to increase revenues of the ski school. Tom Stein, one of the part-time PSIA instructors, suggested the 5 minute ski tip.

Keeping in mind the very limited snow, customers paid a price to ski on the limited terrain and that terrain didn't need a bunch of instructors clogging up the trails while training. So, the staff broke into teams of 2 instructors per ski run and skied in and around the customers and offered them a ski tip or two, then gave them business cards and encouraged them to take a lesson.

With the limited early season snowfall, a challenge from the Ski School Director to come up with creative ideas for increasing business encouraged "Father Bill" to consider creating a program to serve older skiers. Father Bill had been a part-time ski patroller at Copper Mountain and had joined the ski school in the 1974-1975 ski season as a part-time instructor together with Tom Stein and Moe Mosley.

Father Bill developed an idea to create a program for older skiers to keep them involved and visiting Copper, and he presented it to Chuck Lewis during the summer of 1976. Chuck gave him the green light to develop a pilot program in an effort to bring senior skiers back to the slopes and keep them there as they grew older.

During the beginning of the 1976/1977 ski season, Father Bill Magill contacted Tom Stein and Moe Mosley and asked them to assist him in the development of the senior skier program to be offered through the Copper Mountain Ski School. While working full-time in businesses around Denver and also fulfilling their Ski School commitments, the three somehow found time at the mountain for numerous discussions, planning meetings, awareness-building with guests and the rest of the Ski School, and beginning the pilot program. They had the full support of Butch Graves, the Ski School Director, and Floyd Bashant, the Supervisor of the Adult Ski School, and worked with other members of the Copper Mountain team to set up the pilot program.

The pilot program started during the ski season of 1976/1977. After initially testing the interest of guests, they created the formal legal organization with a meeting held on January 18, 1978. The original charter of the Over the Hill Gang Ski Team, Inc., formed as a Colorado non-profit corporation in 1978, stated, "The purpose of the organization is to promote the physical and mental health of members over the age of 45 by providing skiing, social, and fraternal activities." While the minimum age was changed to age 50 eighteen months later, the members that joined that first season built a lasting organization that has gone on to serve decades of senior skiers at Copper Mountain and beyond.

The initial board members were Father Bill, Tom Stein, and Moe Mosley. Numerous board meetings and general meetings were held at Copper Mountain during that founding ski season. After the ski season, morning meetings were held at Elly May's Kitchen in Denver.

The Charter Member meeting was at KOA radio station on the evening of April 19, 1978 with the assistance of Joey Day, President of KOA. 15 people were invited, but 17 showed up!

During the meeting, those present set the membership fee at $10.00. Bill, Moe, and Tom contributed $100 each to support the initial structure of the Over the Hill Gang, and the program was off to the races.

After the meeting, Bill suggested naming the program "Over the Hill Gang." The name "Over the Hill Gang Ski Team of Copper Mountain" appealed to Tom and Moe, as well. But, not so fast—that name had a hurdle to jump from the NFL!

A few years earlier, George Allen, former Head Coach of the NFL's Los Angeles Rams, had left LA and taken over the Washington Redskins as Head Coach and General Manager after Vince Lombardi retired. Mr. Allen had registered the name "The Over the Hill Gang" when the media branded the Redskins with it for their combination of advancing years and a sassy, nasty, and very experienced approach to football.

Since the Copper Mountain team liked the name so much, Tom contacted George Allen and the Washington Redskins in an effort to obtain their permission to use the name. Over the course of conversations, the team and Mr. Allen agreed to allow the new program to use the name, and so, thanks to the generosity of an NFL team and its coach, the name which has now persisted for almost 40 years became official.

At a board meeting on the morning of 9/12/1978, at Elly May's Kitchen, the board approved the Articles of Incorporation and filed them as of that date, making the organization official. The board also approved giving the founders authority to discuss arrangements with Copper Mountain management for the 1978-79 ski season.

Shortly thereafter, Father Bill approached the Demetre company to ask if they would create ski sweaters for the

OHG Ski Team, since Demetre made the USA Olympic Ski Team sweaters. Demetre agreed, so the first OHG sweaters were soon on their way.

At the same time, Moe visited with Physicians Services, Inc. and Personal Medical Inventory, Inc. to see if they would provide medical I.D. cards or tags for members. At the general meetings on December 6 & 9, 1978 he let the members know that they would have access to medical information for all members to have in case of emergency. This is one of many examples of the diversity of skills and focus displayed by the founders, which, in turn, created a unique and lasting foundation.

Those original three part-time PSIA (Professional Ski Instructors of America) ski instructors from Copper Mountain (Father Bill Magill, Tom Stein, and Moe Mosley) although from different cultures, industries, education, and experience, created an exceptionally strong management team to guide the fledgling organization. Each had certain skills and abilities that complemented the others and benefitted the entire program. Many of their original approaches and the foundation they created have been in use for more than 40 years.

While the people who participated as members and staff in those early years were key to the organization's success, the mountain itself had—and continues to have—such spirit and strength that it captured the love and respect of those who experienced it first-hand. As a result, it created a fusion of skiers and mountain, nature and humanity that drew those who were in love with the alpine splendor. The mountain brought a passion to all members of the Copper Mountain team, with ski patrol and instructor staff wanting to make the resort successful by committing to exceptional quality which was recognized across the industry.

The three founding part-time instructors were caught up in that spirit, and with their passion, respect, and love for the mountain that offered its white cape for the joyful experience of skiers.

KEY VALUES

From the beginning, the program and its founders recognized fundamental values for the Over the Hill Gang: it was a non-profit organization and its purpose would always be to promote the physical and mental health of members over 50 by providing skiing, social, and fraternal activities.

In addition, the organization was structured with the following provisions:

- The Original Board Members (the Initial Directors) had first right of refusal upon the sale of any portion of the corporation; and

- If and when ownership of the corporation was transferred, the new owners would identify in their marketing and promotional materials that the organization was founded by three part-time PSIA ski instructors from Copper Mountain, Colorado

Being a legal corporation, as of October 24, 1978, the OHG was ready for the 1978/79 ski season.

Business plans were in place, and when the three founders (who formed the board in the early days) reviewed the arrangement with Chuck Lewis, they had agreed to limit membership to only 25 people in the first year. However, the Charter Membership list had fifty-one members! As a result, the board met with Chuck to explain the unforeseen initial interest and the resulting size of membership.

Chuck expressed his concerns about controlling the growth of a program that could fill the mountain at a discount while taking the quality skiing experience from the public who would be paying full price. He wanted a quality program that worked together with the skiing public, but he also understood the value of the strong interest, and so, after consideration, he agreed to the fifty-one members, recognizing that, although Copper Mountain was a ski business, he wanted quality *and* the highest levels of customer service.

The first official day of the Over the Hill Gang Ski Team of Copper Mountain was December 6, 1978 and it went off without a hitch.

GROWTH

After creating the charter and holding the first official ski day, the three part-time ski instructors built a business foundation and a diagram that they used for marketing and explaining the program. The diagram shows a see-through ball with a triangle supporting it from the inside. They would describe how anyone could hit, roll, or kick the ball, but as long as the triangle stays intact, the ball will remain and there will be a strong and growing program. However, if one of the triangle legs weakens or breaks away, the program becomes unbalanced and will deteriorate.

The diagram tells the story: There are three parts to the Over the Hill Gang Copper Mountain:

- The Mountain—Which supports the members and guides;

- The Membership—Who supports the mountain and guides;

- The Guides—Who support the members and the mountain. They are the energy behind the program.

All three have to remain in balance for the program to thrive into the future.

The leadership of the OHG continuously reviewed the activities and events of the program. During the 1978/ 79 ski season, they reviewed problem areas that were encountered with the organization and Copper Mountain, complaints by members, complaints by the mountain management, a review of the previous season and a draft of a marketing report, together with a review of the financial position of the organization, the establishments of summer activities, an increase in dues for the 1979/80 ski season to $35.00 with the addition of a 50% reduction for all members age 65 and over if they chose to accept the discount.

Moe Mosley completed the 1978/79 Market Report, which included a member and market survey. He presented a written report for review to the Directors at the first summer function. These Market Reports were produced each summer for the first five years of the OHG, although Chuck Lewis only asked for 4 of the 5 reports.

As a summertime continuation of the relationships made during the winter season, the OHG held tennis and golf tournaments and a picnic at Copper Mountain on June 29, 1979. Tom made the arrangements, Bill wrote the newsletter announcing the dates of activities, and Moe obtained the awards. Later that summer on July 21, 1979, the OHG held a gathering for mountain hiking and climbing.

At the July 18, 1979 board meeting, the board reviewed, discussed, and approved the following:

- August and September 1979 activities;
- The design, cost, and proposal (with approval from Copper Mountain) to use the Copper Mountain logo on materials used by the Over the Hill Gang Ski Team;
- Arm bands;
- A reduction in the size of groups skiing, since there were concerns that the groups had become too large;
- Review of the instructors who could possibly be used when needed for the Over the Hill Gang Ski Team;

- A discussion of base pay vs. passes for the guides. Later, the founders discussed the issue with Mountain management and the OHG started using ski passes as compensation for each day worked.

Also at that meeting, the board and members approved the design for an OHG pin that looked very similar to the PSIA certification pins. They also approved the purchase of 225 pins with the names of the member to be printed on them as well as the purchase of 225 arm bands.

The Over the Hill Gang Ski Team at Cooper Mountain took off rapidly. Word quickly spread and membership grew. The resort management held growth in check with yearly limits, but the OHG went from 50 to 100 members virtually overnight.

With the growth, the board approached the Ski School with a request to jointly choose certain instructors to be used beginning with the next season to keep the ski group sizes between 10 and 12 skiers. After the approval to invite specific instructors, the founders talked with each instructor to see if they had an interest in working with the OHG for the upcoming season.

The 1979/80 ski season was a great year for the OHG: the program doubled in membership and the skill level of the skiers joining was very high, even including former ski instructors, ski patrollers, powder hounds, and racers. The team members were like little kids in a candy store. The Mountain wasn't busy, so the OHG, as a group, certainly got out-of-control from time-to-time, not considering either their age or their position in the community. When the mountain management discovered that there were times when guides had 20-27 members in a guided group—far too many people for one guide to handle—Ski School Director Butch Graves, together with Adult Ski School Supervisors, Floyd Bashant and Don Coleman, pitched in and loaned the OHG some of the top instructors and supervisors from the Ski School to ski with and guide the groups. Some of those new guides were former racers, PSIA Examiners (the coaches and graders of instructors as they work their way through certification), and Supervisors of the Ski School.

MEMBERSHIP

The charter members of the OHG were:

Mardee Birchfield	Dorie Callender
Lew Birchfield	John Clay
Libby Bortz	Lorraine Crawford
Alan Bortz	Jack Crawford
Sam Callender	Mary Dailey
Kathy Callender	Joel Day
Galen Callender	Randy Erwin
Jim Callender	R. Flater

Bob Freeman	Don Raymond
Sam Jenkins	Patricia Ronald
Howard Johnston	Dick Ronald
A.W. Kurth	Mary Lee Ross
Jim Leibold	Ken Ross
Angela Leibold	Dick Sanders
Harold Leight	Joe Sanders
Carol Leight	Don Schiff
Ron Lemon	Ed Small
Maggie Lemon	Arthur Snyder
Tom Macey	Ellen Snyder
Nancy Macey	Floyd Stearns
Dave MacKenzie	Janet Stears
Janet MacKenzie	Tom Stein
Bill Magill	Pauline Stein
Jerry "Moe" Mosley	Dee Toscano
Dee Mosley	Jim Toscano
Rya Neslund	Earl Wilson
Elsie Pomponio	Dottie Wilson
Frank Pomponio	

Location for Charter Members:

Those early members came not only from Colorado, but a few were from other spots in the Midwest:

CITY	NUMBER OF FOUNDING MEMBERS
Denver, CO	20
Englewood, CO	10
Littleton, CO	9

CITY	NUMBER OF FOUNDING MEMBERS
Golden, CO	4
Wheat Ridge, CO	4
Arvada, CO	3
Chicago, IL	2
Lakewood, CO	1
Gering, NE	1
Geddard, KS	1

GUIDES

The guides have always been one of the pillars of the organization; one leg of the structural triangle of the foundation of the OHG.

The first ski school members appointed jointly by the Founders and Ski School staff were Jim and Marty Lincoln, a husband and wife team whose son, Ed, joined the guide staff later. As the program continued to grow, the second instructor chosen was Winnie Johnson and the third was Joe Stanski.

With that initial set of guides, the program continued to grow, and the next set of guides jointly appointed were:

Fred Ammer

Vino Anthony

Lynda Collins

Bill Douglas

Tom Henderson

Bob Jackson

Jim Johnson

Chuck Lisle

Tammy Tharatt

Doug Trieste

Due to size of the groups, when the program needed assistance on the hill in the beginning years, the program used many ski school staff members, such as supervisors, racing coaches, and PSIA examiners to guide. Among them were:

<table>
<tr><td>Jay Abott</td><td>Mark Jones</td></tr>
<tr><td>Floyd Bashant</td><td>Mike Klysa</td></tr>
<tr><td>Don Coleman</td><td>Larry Lash</td></tr>
<tr><td>Moe Dixon</td><td>Bob Layton</td></tr>
<tr><td>Jim Galbreath</td><td>Craig McNeil</td></tr>
<tr><td>Butch Graves</td><td>Dave Sanctuary</td></tr>
<tr><td>Dean Jones</td><td></td></tr>
</table>

Bill Sloatman (nicknamed "Slot-car", a name also given to one of Copper Mountain's ski runs)

For the 1982-83 ski season the program added the following guides:

Kristi Eastman Anderson
Chris Cocallas
Mike Pogliano (Pog)
Melinda Van Gundy

Shortly after that, the program added:

<table>
<tr><td>Mark Addison</td><td>Doug Erickson</td></tr>
<tr><td>Polly Addison</td><td>Mark Gidney</td></tr>
<tr><td>Ray Allen</td><td>Dick Guyer</td></tr>
<tr><td>Glen Anderson</td><td>Rob Hill</td></tr>
<tr><td>Dodi Cariaso</td><td>Mike Homier</td></tr>
<tr><td>Steve Combs</td><td>Rich Hopper</td></tr>
<tr><td>Holly Emrick</td><td>Gene Jencsok</td></tr>
<tr><td>Ken Emrick</td><td>Stephan Jencsok</td></tr>
</table>

Mike Kelley	Joe Quarantillo
Chuck Levi	Tom Stein, Jr.
Bud Monk	Carl Weller
René Moser	Ken Zimmerman

When Dick Guyer joined the Guides, he brought with him decades of experience as a ski patroller, including a period as Patrol Director at Nubs Nob in Michigan. His expansion to guiding and teaching underscored his love of the sport and sharing it with as many people as he could. Into his seventies, two knee replacements (done on the same day!), fighting off cancer, and clawing his way back to skiing well, his smile, laughter, and contagious spirit encourages the members and other guides every day.

All the guides were chosen for their excellent interpersonal skills and their superior skiing ability. Their focus on providing both excellent ski experiences and ski instruction for the members created a unique environment unparalleled in recreational skiing. As the program expanded, the team gave many talks to explain the program and promote it. One time, during a talk at a business luncheon in Denver, one of the program founders showed the names of the guides that worked (that is, skied) with the program, stating, "This is one hell of a lot of great skier talent for a new ski area to have, let alone a simple senior ski program." The self-effacing humor resonated with these listeners there and at other events, and the program continued to grow.

During the years the three founders owned the organization, they spoke about it at a number of functions. Later, after Copper Mountain assumed ownership of the program in 1986, the membership continued meeting the challenge of speaking about and promoting the program. These talks helped market the program to a broad range of skiers.

The last known outside talk about the Copper OHG program was by Dick Masica, officer of the Copper Mountain OHG Advisory Board, on July 27, 2004.

Many others joined the ranks of the guides over the years, including those who excelled at snowboarding, telemark, and Nordic skiing. Dick Guyer with Stephan Jencsok and Gene Jencsok, and others, worked together to get a solid group of the members involved with Nordic skiing, for example.

Best-selling author, CEO, and internationally celebrated leadership advisor Dr. Lance Secretan (and co-author of this book) was a guide for several years. Author Steve Hultquist (also a co-author of this book) has been a guide since 2003, and his first book ("Open Your Heart with Skiing, Mastering Life Through Love of the Turns," published in 2007) includes many anecdotes from OHG days.

Collaboration with the Colorado Ski Education Foundation

The Colorado Ski Education Foundation of Copper Mountain, an organization that provided scholarships to hopeful ski racers for the benefit of the U.S. Ski Team, approached the OHG membership and board through Chuck Lewis to see if the Over the Hill Gang Ski Team would be interested in lending assistance to the Education Foundation program.

After consideration, the members of the program decided to support the foundation and the skiers it chose to sponsor. They raised money to assist racers in need and to help offset the foundation's expenses. The OHG members also worked the races to eliminate expense and keep operating costs as low as possible.

The racers were put up in quarters at Copper Mountain for the season, as well.

After the first season, the OHG members and board reviewed their support of the racing program. They were delighted to find that the educational working relationship with the Summit County Education System was very good, the coaching was excellent, the Mountain and the Racing Foundation worked well together, the food was good, and the program was meeting its goals.

Except for one thing: the living and studying quarters.

The racers were staying in a condo without a private room for sleeping and studying. To grow the program, the Foundation, the Mountain, and the OHG would have to find a better living environment for the racers. However, the program already represented substantial cost for the sponsors, and the living quarters available at Copper Mountain were insufficient as accommodations for young racers.

The members involved struggled to find a solution to this challenge. They were committed to skiing and to supporting the young racers and wanted to find a way to make a difference. In the end, though, they recommended to Chuck Lewis that the program be closed at the end of the season with the racers and coaches transferring into other ski foundations around the country, including both Vail and Aspen.

Steady Growth

During the 1979, 1980, and 1981 seasons, the OHG had controlled growth above the planned membership pace. The members enjoyed the opportunities to ski with other skiers of their generation at their own levels and with exceptional guidance and skiing insights from world-class instructors. Every year there were surprises and unexpected incidents, typical for a growing organization, but in February 1981, the program experienced a challenge and shock when founding board member Tom Stein had a heart attack on the hill just before taking a group out to ski. The ski patrol responded quickly and provided their usual high level of professional intervention during this emergency. Tom survived his on-snow scare and continued skiing with the OHG for many more years.

In early 1981, the board discussed the potential of changing the organization from non-profit to a for-profit corporation. However, by August, the founders decided that doing so would result in a negative impact on the guide staff, so elected to retain the organization's non-profit status.

Starting with the 1980/81 season, the Over the Hill Gang Ski Team of Copper Mountain received considerable press coverage and requests for TV interviews from around the Country.

Typically, the coverage was good for Copper Mountain and the program, but not so much for the camera crews and journalists who had a hard time keeping up with the OHG groups they were covering at Copper! Those crews expected the "old people" to be picking their ways slowly down extremely easy terrain, yet nothing was further from the truth. The members represented a wide range of abilities from low-end "No Worries" skiers to high end "Incline" skiers who hiked up the mountain, seeking fresh powder turns and giving every other skier on the mountain a run for their money.

There were more than 150 members each time the cameras visited the program, and some of the videos filmed at that time still exist.

The Copper Mountain Over the Hill Gang Ski Team helped to sponsor a gala benefit for the Colorado Ski Museum in October, 1981 attended by more than 250 people for the dinner and over 300 for the movie that followed.

That spring, the Copper Mountain OHG coordinated a highway cleanup along I-70 with the Colorado Department of Transportation (CDOT), and the program has continued to serve Summit County and the State of Colorado by helping to clean up the highway each spring ever since.

The members of the OHG program became deeply connected to Copper Mountain as they continued skiing the mountain every year, becoming more and more integrated with the life-pulse of the resort. As they did so, members came up with creative ideas to help the resort serve its other guests. One of the ideas was to establish an Ambassador program to welcome and serve Copper Mountain guests—a program that exists and thrives to this day. The resort created the program, and even today, OHG members and guides are among those who volunteer with the Ambassadors.

During the early years of the OHG program, OHG guides received first aid and CPR training to help them in their role leading groups of skiers around the mountain.

The Copper Mountain OHG Program had its structure, foundation, and business operation in place. The members and board were invited to speak about the OHG program by travel agencies and airlines, creating even more opportunity to show senior skiers the opportunity available to continue enjoying sliding on snow with friends that they could meet on the mountain at Copper.

In the early part of the 1981 ski year, Copper Mountain OHG entered a joint venture with United, Frontier, and Continental Airlines, together with Travel Agencies, to transport 100 skiers on each airline to Denver. The Copper Mountain OHG bused each group to Copper Mountain.

As part of the promotion, the team discussed with the airlines the possibility of building a snow slope at the airport so that OHG guides and guests would ski down as they arrived and departed using the ultra-short GLM (Graduated Length Method) skis that were being used so successfully in ski schools at the time. Cliff Taylor, inventor of the GLM, which used shorter skis to make learning easier for new skiers, taught at Copper Mountain and worked in the Real Estate Department.

While wacky and fun, cooler heads prevailed, and the guests deplaned in the usual way.

The trips were held in January, February, and March of 1982, and were very successful due to the commitment and assistance received from the Copper Mountain guides, Ski School staff, and the OHG founders who all spent many long days and nights making sure the guests all had a wonderful time.

The OHG of Copper Mountain charged $50.00 for each of the visiting participants' membership, which covered the transportation to and from Copper Mountain, an introduction breakfast, and a dinner on the final evening. The balance of the expenses for room and board, ski school lessons, mountain ski passes, rentals, and so on, were paid by the visitors through their travel agent or directly to Copper Mountain.

These trips introduced many more senior skiers to Copper Mountain and the idea of skiing together with a group of contemporaries, enjoying the mountain experience and the connection with one another. It contributed to the growth of the Copper Mountain program while also leading to a rapid expansion of the program beyond the resort of Copper Mountain.

THE EARLY YEARS AS TOLD BY
BYRON "BUTCH" GRAVES

I was Copper Mountain Ski School Director at the very beginning of the OHG Program. I started at Copper Mountain as the Adult Ski School Supervisor in 1972 after being the Ski School Director at an area called Hidden Valley, and I was also a PSIA Examiner. I worked with Jim Isham to start building a highly-qualified ski school until 1974 when I became Ski School Director and continued the building process.

I met Bill Magill in 1973 when he was on the Copper Mountain Ski Patrol and requested that he tryout to become a member of the Instructor Staff in the 1974-75 season. Our Ski School Management Staff had continued recruiting qualified and experienced staff, and during the 1974-75 season we hired about 10 new Instructors, with Tom Stein, Moe Mosley, and Bill Magill being a part of the hiring clinic.

The Ski School Management Staff asked the entire Ski School to come up with ideas to improve revenue performance on the hill and the bottom line. As I look back, I realize that those three founders had a great combination of business skills, motivation, and experience. In a way, it was a perfect team.

- "Father Bill" Magill was the Reverend at St Luke's Episcopal Church and loved to speak to groups.

- Tom Stein was the Director of Communications at the University of Colorado and had many friends in the press, radio, and television.

- Moe Mosley was a business consultant in the Health & Welfare Industry who then moved to an International Consulting Actuarial Firm.

Because of this combination, the Program was not built out of their hip pockets. It was a very structured business from the start. All the meetings were held at Copper Mountain during the Ski Season and Floyd Bashant and I were always invited. As time passed, Floyd and I discovered what we were up against with the founders and the program itself.

One Saturday, while riding the American Flyer lift, Floyd and I were checking on Ski School classes and we spotted one of the OHG Founders guiding 22 OHG members down that crowded run. Floyd said "we've got to split that group and give the guide a helping hand." I suggested to Floyd, "No, let's watch for a minute and see how he is going to move and control that size of group down that run." You see, we had a great bunch of instructors in those early years who were all PSIA trained and knew the proper PSIA Ski Manual procedures, but each of those instructors had their own little bag of tricks that we in management sometimes forgot they had.

That group made it down the mountain safe and sound for three runs that I know about, without any accidents or other events. However, at the end of the day we had a meeting with the three founders and jointly selected Jim and Marty Lincoln of our Instructor Staff to become Guides for the OHG Program to help shrink the group sizes.

Right behind Jim and Marty, we recruited Winnie Johnson and Joe Stanski from our instructor Staff to guide for the OHG Program.

After I left Copper Mountain, I took over the full time Race Program at Vail, but stayed in contact with the Program. When I left Vail, I moved to Steamboat Springs as Ski School Director and continued to stay in contact and follow the developments of the OHG and attended the OHG 25th Reunion.

Reviewing the history as I know it, those three Founders were ahead of themselves and they had everything in proper business order:

- A Founder who likes public speaking (to sell the Program).

- A Founder who had major marketing contacts at newspapers, radio, trade press, and TV.
- A Founder with business and legal experience.

Once those three items were covered they only needed two additional items to cover:

- A mountain (Copper was young, hungry, and world-class), and
- A strong Certified PSIA Ski School with instructors that could change from teaching to building better skiers with their bag of 5-minute ski tips to improve the member's skiing skills and ability level.

These three Founders and the Program had their ups and downs, but they never stopped moving and believing in how much the Program was needed. They could be a handful to deal with at times, but they were always fun to watch in the progress!

Byron "Butch" Graves

PM MAGAZINE

Prior to the expansion of the Over the Hill Gang vision beyond Copper Mountain, the TV show PM Magazine visited Copper to ski with the Gang for a day. They interviewed members as well as Father Bill and Tom Stein. Moe was on-camera, but, as he often does, avoided being interviewed.

One of the members, George Winter, spoke for many Over the Hill Gang members over the years when he said, "I was skiing by myself, and didn't like it." The host observed that, "It's never too late to learn," and that "many members have started skiing in their 40s, 50s, and even later in life".

During the show, of course, the members skied so fast and so well that the cameramen couldn't keep up, so the producers hired members of Warren Miller's on-snow crew to do the camera work. During one scene, the members overtook the on-camera host, spraying him with snow as they passed him, and in another, one of the grandmothers showed her skills at quilting before throwing her work to the snow and skiing off, "laying them low!"

That year, the members won over 170 NASTAR medals, demonstrating their on-snow skills, and, as founder Tom Stein said, they found, "not a fountain of youth, but a mountain of youth!" Shortly after the original local broadcast, it was re-broadcast nationally, and supported the early expansion beyond Copper Mountain.

EXPANSION BEYOND COPPER MOUNTAIN

In 1981, the OHG International was developed. The members of the Copper Mountain Over the Hill Gang began expanding their vision of senior skiing to other resorts. Many of the original members had been regular guests at Winter Park and began organizing visits there and to other mountains as an opportunity to expand their enjoyment of a variety of mountains and to grow as skiers and friends.

These activities led to the development of the organization into The Over the Hill Gang International and the Winter Park SkiMeisters over the next few years.

THE OVER THE HILL GANG INTERNATIONAL

The original group of the Copper Mountain OHG Skiers was a very close and tight-knit group. Many of them had come to the OHG from Winter Park, where OHG co-founder Tom Stein had been a ski instructor for the Eskimo Club for five years, and was a friend and neighbor of Jerry Groswold, the President of Winter Park at the time.

During the time that Tom was at the Eskimo Club, Max Dercum had started the ski school for the new Keystone Ski Area. Tom left Winter Park and became a part time instructor for three years at Keystone prior to the formation of the Copper Mountain Ski School which began by hiring about 40 full- and part-time ski instructors, including Tom Stein, Moe Mosley and Bill Magill, who was with Copper Mountain Ski Patrol before joining the ski school.

These other ski resorts are also home to a tight-knit community of snowsports industry professionals in the Colorado Rocky Mountains.

Those outside parties watched closely as Father Bill, Tom, and Moe created the strong business foundation for the OHG and a working structure for a senior ski program. After observing the OHG's progress, Mr. Groswold made several approaches to Tom Stein, inviting him to start a program at Winter Park. The three OHG founders wanted to help start the program at Winter Park, but with their full-time careers and (theoretically) part-time commitment to Copper and the Copper Mountain OHG, their hands and plates were more than full.

However, with the media attention gained by the Copper Mountain OHG, the original founders developed the OHG International (OHGI) in 1981 with a view to forming OHG chapters at other ski areas. The OHGI also enabled the creation of chapters that were not affiliated with a particular resort and even some that were not located in the mountains. Clubs could choose different venues by negotiating with ski areas separately. With the help of Jerry Groswold, the first international chapter was formed at Winter Park, Colorado in 1982.

At the time, the Copper Mountain OHG had more than 250 members. A group of about 60 members who had been Winter Park skiers before joining the Copper Mountain OHG migrated back to Winter Park because it was more convenient for them, enabling them to have smaller guided groups.

The on-snow experience of the Over the Hill Gang International at Winter Park began with skiers on the hill December 19th, 1982.

During the years that followed, the Winter Park organization grew into a strong, independent senior ski program. In 1983 the Winter Park Chapter of the OHG International, Inc. had 39 members and 5 guides. In 1984, Rosie May was elected the first President and Tom Kilroy, a PSIA certified ski instructor and dentist from Illinois, and an original guide with the Copper Mountain OHG, was one of the first guides for the Winter Park Group and became their first Director of Skiing. In the Fall of 1984, the group published the first issue of their newsletter, *Winter Park Flurries*.

Between 1982 and April 1985, the OHG International,

Inc. built chapters located and associated with local ski areas as well as independent chapters which negotiated agreements with many different mountains. The OHGI Agreement helped to guide the participant organizations under the OHG Guidelines.

As the OHGI program expanded, the OHG founders became interested in using the famous Grant Wood painting, *American Gothic*, as their trademark for the OHGI. They realized they would need to obtain permission to use it in an altered state—they envisioned the couple holding skis instead of a pitchfork!

To obtain permission, Tom Stein visited the Chicago Art Museum, the owners of the original Grant Wood painting. The museum introduced Tom to Nan Graham, Grant Wood's sister, a wonderful lady of 85 years young who was residing in a nursing home. Tom went to visit her.

Mrs. Graham wanted to see a copy of the drawing before giving permission for its use. As Tom showed it to her and explained the purpose of the OHG, she became excited at the prospect of having the logo support an organization for active seniors, and gave the OHGI written permission for its use. As a result of her generosity, she became an honorary member of the OHG International, an honor also bestowed later to President Ford and Pope John XXIII.

After Mrs. Graham provided the written permission to use the altered painting, Tom asked if the house in the background of the original was their childhood home. She looked at Tom with a sparkle in her eyes and a chuckle on her lips and said, "Oh no, that was a house of illegal activity of women and men—a whore house!"

NEW OWNERSHIP

In April 1985, assets of the OHG International were purchased from Tom Stein by Bill Vandersluis, including the trademark and federally protected logos. Since he had not previously been involved with the ski industry, Mr. Vandersluis created a corporation called Over Corp and invited the following directors and advisory board members:

- Wm. J. Vandersluis, Chairman
- Minetta A. Miller, Coordinating Director
- Earl E. Clark, Events Director (10th Mountain Division)
- A.J. McKenna, Communications Director (10th Mountain Division)
- Tom Stein, Senior Ski Advisor

A few months after the original purchase, the Over Corp purchased the OHGI from Mr. Vandersluis for the exact same price that it had been previously purchased from Tom Stein, transferring ownership to a corporation for the first time, and later Mr. Vandersluis stepped down, selling his share to the remaining board members.

In 1985, the official name was "The Over the Hill Gang of Denver International" with 200 members.

DENNIS AND SHERRI BEASLEY

Starting in 1991 The OHGI experienced dramatic growth under the guidance of Dennis and Sherri Beasley, both of whom came from broad and capable backgrounds.

Dennis Beasley, a 5th generation Coloradan, was born in Silverton, Colorado, the fifth highest town in the United States. Since his family were all westerners, being outdoors was a natural part of his life. He doesn't even remember learning to ski since it happened when he was so young! Dennis graduated from high school in Westminster, Colorado, obtaining his undergraduate degree in forestry from Colorado State University while skiing for both his high school and college ski teams as well as running ski trips for them.

Sherrie was born in Nebraska and then moved to Cheyenne, Wyoming, attending 9 years of school there before moving to Westminster, Colorado, where she graduated from high school—and met Dennis! She went on to Colorado State also, but after a year was swept off her feet and married Dennis. She then concentrated on helping him get through school by working so he could finish. When Dennis was a senior, their daughter, Denise, who later became General Manager for Over the Hill Gang, International, was born.

In addition to the outdoors, Dennis had always had a love of flying, gained from his father, who flew in WWII. After Dennis graduated, he worked for the US Forest Service, but still yearned to fly, so he entered the Air Force with a commission from Officer's Training School. Soon after, their son, Kris, was born, and he eventually became a Colonel in the US Air Force—the result of inheriting the family tradition for a love of flying. For thirty years, Dennis flew C-130's, serving in the Communications/Computer wing of the Air Force, ultimately retiring as a

Brigadier General. Sherrie loved the lifestyle—even the 20 moves—because of the many interesting people and travel opportunities they experienced.

Unlike Dennis, who grew up skiing, Sherrie didn't begin until the children were small. However, it soon became the family sport and a way of life. During their 3 year tour in Japan, the Beasleys helped run the largest American/International ski club in the country, planning trips every week during ski season for the group. When stationed in Europe, they skied all over the Alps and as often as possible.

When Dennis was transferred to the Pentagon in 1985, Sherrie, who had been working in the travel industry for a few years, went to work for a company called Any Mountain Tours, a ski travel company. During that time, by chance, she became a travel planner for Over the Hill Gang International, which was under Earl Clark's leadership. She was totally enthralled with this group of wonderful, active, senior skiers and decided that it would be a great way to spend their senior years. As soon as Dennis turned 50, they joined as members and began skiing with the Over the Hill Gang, beginning a decades-long relationship with the organization.

When Earl Clark began looking for someone to take over the group so he could retire, he approached the Beasleys. The timing was good, since Dennis was getting ready to retire from the Air Force and the Beasleys wanted to return to Colorado. They took over in November, 1991. With approximately 1200 members, the Beasleys set their sights on developing an organization that would serve senior skiers in many ways. Their goal of providing senior skiers with ski companions that would last later into life involved many facets: discounts, ski days with guides, and trips. Their mission was to provide superb customer service to all the members, all the time, so they could achieve those goals.

Over the 15 years of the Beasley's involvement in Over the Hill Gang International (OHGI), the organization grew to over 7,200 members, member benefits and discounts available grew significantly, and the number of trips offered grew from 6 to over 35 each year.

What did the members get out of all that? They received the means and encouragement to continue skiing and remain active, to visit new places and enjoy new experiences with others who had the same interests and vitality, and perhaps most importantly, it afforded them the opportunity to meet many other like-minded people, as evidenced by the many groups of friends formed within OHGI. The Beasleys have been amazed at the networks and interconnections that have been formed among the members who have met each other on OHGI trips. It is one of the single biggest and best benefits created by OHGI.

What did the Beasleys get out of OHGI? In the course of hosting over 145 OHGI trips around the world, attending member meetings, and joining ski days, they have met thousands of great people they would never have met otherwise, and made friendships that they will treasure forever. Furthermore, they have experienced the joy of providing a great service with a safe, comfortable environment for seniors, both married and single, while continuing to stay active, participating in a sport that many people abandoned before reaching the age of 40.

Some other less obvious benefits they received were the honor of acting as unofficial spokespeople for senior skiers, representing them to the ski and adventure industry, and attempting to influence the industry to not overlook this affluent and active population. They also harnessed their creative and entrepreneurial talents, running their own business, publishing newsletters and catalogs, and most importantly, creating something of value. They say it was a great experience with great people.

As more and more baby boomers face retirement and life after 50, the need for an organization such as OHGI will continue to grow, as long as it meets the needs of its members and keeps focused on its core values of camaraderie, benefits, and comfortable, worry-free travel. This is the legacy the Beasleys have contributed to skiing.

THE SKIMEISTERS

The Winter Park Chapter of the Over the Hill Gang International, Inc. was formed in August 1984 as the first OHGI chapter, and it was registered as a Colorado non-profit corporation. The officers were: President, Rosie May, Vice-President, Eames Yates, Secretary, Maggie Lemon, Treasurer, Mary Jessen. The Directors were Nancy Lamphere, Pete Franklin, Norma Tucker, Bob and Ann Beck. Norm Anderson was appointed Mountain Man (the liaison to Winter Park). Other coordinators were: Events —Bill Wegert, Membership—Shirley Wegert, Social— Rosie May, Cross-Country—Rodger and Karen Foreman.

At this time, there were 38 members and 5 guides. The discounted lift ticket for the OHGI was $19.

At the annual meeting in October 1988, the motion of seceding from Over the Hill Gang International was put to the membership. After lengthy and, at times, heated discussion, the membership voted to separate from International. The board decided to change its name to prevent any difficulty with OHGI. The name SkiMeisters, suggested by Ernie Jessen, was accepted.

Consulting a commercial artist for the logo design was considered, and Ann Beck advised that her brother was an artist and could be persuaded to help them. The Nordic Snow God Ullr was featured on some medallions the ladies wore, so Ullr was used as a model. The original drawing shows him skiing to the left, which didn't look right on stationery, so he was flipped by the printer. That is the story of how SkiMeisters came to be.

The first set of bylaws for The SkiMeisters was developed by Mary Jessen and Norma Tucker, and in October, 1988 the organization published the premier issue of *SkiMeisters Flurries*, edited by Ernie Jessen.

The membership of SkiMeisters grew rapidly, from 194 members in 1989 to 300 in 1994, and then was capped at 400 members in 1995 at the request of Winter Park, and the minimum age was raised to 55.

The club continues to offer many wonderful opportunities, and all SkiMeisters are encouraged to get involved. The officers and board are constantly looking for enthusiastic motivated individuals to lead trips, organize activities, and provide club leadership, and who are dedicated to making SkiMeisters the best it can be.

Members have also organized non-sanctioned domestic and international events such as cruises; bike, canoe, and hiking trips; and Spanish language immersion trips to Mexico.

SkiMeisters has many social events which are now held in public locations. However, when the group was smaller, many of the members generously hosted activities in their homes and yards. This is no longer possible due to the size of the organization.

The SkiMeisters of Winter Park have great special events, programs, and communications to offer their membership, and offer a comprehensive handbook.

SKIMEISTER SPECIAL EVENTS

The Special Events for each season are planned by a Supervisor of Special Events. In the past, these have included events like:

- Ski Improvement Days with lessons given by Winter Park instructors in a small-group lesson setting

- Telemark Lesson Day with lessons given by Winter Park instructors in a small-group lesson setting

- Lunch Days when SkiMeisters provides lunch for members at the Snoasis.

- NASTAR Days with SkiMeisters providing two timed runs for each participating member. SkiMeisters awards ribbons for the first, second, and third place racers on each of the three days.

- Ski Poker Days when boxes containing poker cards are taped to trees near the top of six lifts. Members pick a card from each of the boxes during the morning. At lunch time at Snoasis, each member shows his or her best five of the six cards and the high hand receives a special gift.

- Crazy Hat Days—on one Sunday, Wednesday, and Thursday during the season, members wear a crazy hat or helmet for fun and laughs on the hill.

SKIING LEVELS

One great advantage of skiing with a senior ski program is being able to ski with skiers of a similar age and ability. Members determine the group with whom they would like to ski each day based on their energy and skill level, physical challenges, and any other factor to allow them to have the best day possible.

There are seven skiing levels for SkiMeisters. Each ski day, the SkiMeisters separate into a number of groups within these skiing levels. On some days, particularly Sundays, there may not be enough skiers to fill all seven levels.

The purpose of the levels is to give members the opportunity to ski in small groups with others of similar ability. Of course, Winter Park is renowned for its excellent bump skiing, so bumps figure very prominently in group selection. The levels are:

1. Ski runs that are groomed. Avoids all bump trails. Skis easy blue slopes and any green slopes. Skis at slow speeds with frequent stops.

2. Ski runs that are groomed, but may ski some powder. Avoids all bump trails. Ski easy and moderate blue slopes. Ski at moderate speeds with several stops.

3. Ski runs that are groomed, but may ski some powder. Avoids all bump trails. Ski any blue and blue-black (and occasionally black) groomed slope. Ski at fast speeds with rare stops.

4. Should be at least a high intermediate skier when on groomed trails, but wants to improve his/her bump technique. The group usually skis a mix of small bumps and groomed trails. Bump runs are skied slowly with frequent stops.

5. Should be at least a high intermediate skier when on groomed trails and at least an intermediate bump skier. The group usually skis a mix of blue-black and moderate black bump trails. Some groomed trails may be mixed in with the bumps. Bump runs are skied slowly with frequent stops.

6. Should be at least an advanced skier. The group skis any black bump trails and generally skis all black trails. Bump runs are skied at moderate speeds with several stops. Seeks powder runs when available.

7. Should be at least an expert bump skier. The group skis all black bump trails, all day, throughout Winter Park Resort. Bump runs are skied at fast speeds with rare stops. Seeks powder runs when available.

Of course, levels may be adjusted from time to time.

THE EVOLUTION OF SKIMEISTERS

During the late Spring of 1988, the Law Firm of Davis Graham & Stubbs provided pro bono services to tidy up the legal and business affairs of the SkiMeisters, with the club making the partner providing the services an honorary member.

The first annual meeting of the restructured SkiMeisters was held on October 20, 1989 at the Lowry Air Force Base Officer's Club where the Copper Mountain OHG had also met for their annual meeting in the early years.

In the early to mid-1980's, both the SkiMeisters and the Copper Mountain OHG group voted to stay independent of the OHGI which was growing separately.

In 1983 the Winter Park group was building membership with 39 members and 5 guides who were Bill Douglas, Ray May, Lee Waldman, Charlie Van Der Mark, and Shirley Wegert. The organization was looking forward to additional growth in the 1984/1985 season.

In those early years, Rob Howell (at a hearty 83 years young!) would appear and ski a day on the slopes. Walt Laub, a 10th Mountain Division Alumnus who was one of the most acrobatic skiers of both the Copper Mountain and Winter Park groups, would light up the mountain doing Reuel Christies and 360s.

In the late 1980's and early 1990's, the Copper Mountain OHG, the SkiMeisters of Winter Park, and the OHG International together had over 8,000 senior skiers enjoying winter sports annually, and they all continued to grow.

On March 8th, 2001, Dick Over, another alumnus of the 10th Mountain Division, brought national attention to Winter Park by contributing to the 26th episode of the Ming Tsai Adventure Cooking Show on National TV. Dick showed Ming how the ski troops prepared food in sub-zero temperatures over a small gasoline stove. Ming, an avid skier, and Dick spent two hours taming the slopes of Parsenn Bowl.

A large part of the success of the SkiMeisters program was and is the group of volunteer guides organized by Norm and Shirley Anderson, followed by Bill and Shirley Weigert in a non-structured plan, based on fun, skier ability, and camaraderie.

And not to be forgotten is Bob Brunson, who didn't discover the joy of skiing until he was 49 years old. However, he will tell you that skiing changed his life. This WWII fighter pilot, who turned 91 in June of 2012, demonstrated the very best of the skiing community. Those in this club and all that know and love him really want to be like Bob when they grow up.

To get a sense of the community and camaraderie of the SkiMeisters, read this senior skier poem published in one of the SkiMeisters newsletters of the 1980s:

Senior Skier

by Tom Greening, from Los Angeles,
reprinted with his permission

This will be the fortieth season
That I've put a pair of skis on.
Will my injured ankle hurt?
Will my senses be alert?
Fall lines seem a whole lot steeper,
Tickets are not getting cheaper,
Winters steadily get colder
Every year that I get older.

Moguls now are big as barns,
And every muscle in me warns
That if I want them to perform
I must always keep them warm,
And so I don an extra sweater
And wonder if perhaps I'd better
Stick to intermediate hills
And forgo the tempting thrills
Of schussing down between the trees
With this pair of wobbly knees.
Why, you ask, do I still ski
When it's plain for all to see
My technique is badly rusted
And my balance can't be trusted?
Why not stay content at home
And write another silly poem?
My answer is, forgive me please,
I have a terminal disease—
Just like a person who's converted
And whom all reason has deserted,
I am a chronic True Believer,
A hopeless victim of Ski Fever.

ADDITIONAL ASPECTS OF SKIMEISTERS

In addition to the SkiMeisters on-snow program, there are other benefits for members, including discounts on ski tuning, after ski parties, special rates on lodging near Winter Park, cross-country skiing program and trips to other cross-country areas, a tennis program, canoe trips, the BikeMeister program, a hiking program, Cruise-

Meisters, the SkiMeisters official publication, "The Flurries", the SkiMeisters website, and email addresses.

MORE SKIMEISTER HISTORY

In the beginning a small group of volunteers established and ran the organization and did the majority of the work, which included maintaining the financial records, publishing the newsletter, managing the membership and waitlist databases, planning the social events and entertainment, and running the varied subgroup activities. Among those selfless volunteers who dedicated years of service to create and maintain the traditions and camaraderie of the group were Mary and Ernie Jessen, Bob and Ann Beck, Rose and Ray May, LoRee Roemer, and Norma Tucker. The early visionaries paved the way for those who followed.

1978—Over the Hill Gang formed at Copper Mountain by part-time PSIA Ski Instructors.

1982—Opening of the Winter Park Chapter of the Over the Hill Gang, first day of skiing with 25 members on December 19th

1983—Winter Park Chapter organized with 39 members, 4 guides.

1984—Rosie May elected first President, Tom Kilroy first Director of Skiing. In the fall, the Winter Park Chapter published the first issue of *Winter Park Flurries*.

1985—Over the Hill Gang Denver with 200 members. Board: Bob & Ann Beck, Pete Franklin, Nancy

Lamphere, Maggie Lemon, Rosie May, Norma Tucker, Eames Yates, Mary Jessen, Treasurer and Membership Chair (19 years!).

1988—Withdrew from OHGI and became SkiMeisters named by Ernie Jessen, logo by Ann Beck's brother. First by-laws by Mary Jessen and Norma Tucker. October first publication of *SkiMeister Flurries* with Editor Ernie Jessen (19 years!).

Initial Members and Guides

Rosemary Ashura
Ann & Bob Beck
Joe Bock
Dick Bowers
Wally Burke
Judy Carpenter
Don Chisholm
Sally & Mack Clayton
Ross Davis
Bill Douglas
Betty & Don Drake
Stu Edmonds
Tom Hardy
Ingrid Hartley
Jim Hensley
Dorothy Herbertson
Naomi & Clair Iverson
Shirley Kerrigan
Estelle (Jay) Langston
Walter Laub

Rosie & Ray May
Adelaide Maier
Beryl & Hank McCleary
Delores Newland
Barbara Norgren
Fred Nyland
Dick Over
Charlie Price
Ursula & William Rader
Mike Schaffner
Dorris Ziolkowski Smith
Jerry Tewell
Norma Tucker
Barbara Tulk
Charlie Van Der Mark
Jim Vine
Lee Waldman
Bud Weisner
Maesel Yelenick

Presidents

Presidents of OHG International at Winter Park

1984–1985   Rosie May
1985–1987   Eames Yates
1987–1988   Bob Beck

Presidents of SkiMeisters

1988–1989   George Laflin
1989–1990   Wally Burke
1990–1991   Jim Vine
1991–1993   Art Shenkin
1993–1994   Jim Hanan
1994–1996   Dave Young
1996–1997   Jim Hanan
1997–1998   Koby Kellog
1998–1999   Bill Urquhart
1999–2000   Jim Svenson
2000–2002   Dick Williams
2002–2004   Ron Slovikowski
2004–2005   Lynn Gadd
2005–2006   Emil Shulsinger
2006–2007   Tom Joy
2007–2008   Roger Chamberlain
2008–2009   Jack Moritz
2009–2010   Janet Limbach
2010–2011   Jim Laney
2011–2012   Janice Mulvany
2012–2013   Richard Loeffler
2013–2014   Beth Murphy

Chuck Lewis, founder and builder of Copper Mountain looking at the site prior to construction of the ski area.

Sunset over Copper Mountain.

(Photo credit: Tripp Fay / Copper Mountain Resort)

Aerial view of Camp Hale 10th Mountain Division Base eight months after construction. December, 1942.

Camp Hale, looking north. December, 1942.

The construction site for Camp Hale, early 1942.

The three founders of the Senior Skiing Program in America. Left to right:
Jerry 'Moe' Mosley, Father Bill Magill, Tom Stein.

Copper Mountain trail map today.

The three founders. Left to right: Tom Stein, Moe Mosley, Father Bill Magill, along with member and advisor, Howard Johnston, wearing OHG sweaters.

Copper Mountain after completions of the building of the ski area.

Women's Gold Run award winners. Left to right: Winnie Johnson, Sara Swain, Jennifer Walker, Kay Geitner.

PEOPLE

AMERICA'S "FIRST SKIER," former President Gerald Ford, recently joined the Over-the-Hill Gang Ski Team International, a 5-year-old, Colorado-based group with chapters in California, the Midwest and New England. A long-time frequenter of Vail and other Colorado resorts, Ford took up skiing many years ago in his native state of Michigan. He and other members of this over-50 ski club are role models for older Americans who have no plans to give up active sports. Team president Tom Stein said that Ford hopes to participate in some of the group's first summer events this May or June.

Gerald Ford

Former President Gerald Ford and Tom Stein discussing his membership and OHG skiing schedule.

Men's Gold Run Award Winners. Left to right: Pete Sowinski, Paul Kresge, Moe Mosley, Harley Van De Wege, Tom Snow.

View from the top of Rendezvous lift.

Stunning aerial view of a beautiful mountain – Copper Mountain.

(Photo credit: Mark Tepsic / Copper Mountain)

The Stories of
the Gang

Every day skiing with the Gang creates stories of snow, sun, mountains, companionship, adventure, and joy. A number of current and former members and guides have shared their stories for this book, offering deeper insights into the experiences of the Over the Hill Gang. To give you an idea of how prolific this group is, the OHG's culture of "ski first, talk later," continues. Through data provided by the "Flaik" GPS monitoring system, we know that in the 2013 season the OHG logged over 42 million vertical feet and over 55,000 miles on Copper Mountain trails, demonstrating how the OHG continues to promote physical and mental health of members 50 and over by providing skiing, social, and fraternal activities.

OHG groups ski, move, and stay warm on the coldest days. Snow safety, terrain openings, and trail conditions are studied and discussed daily.

Since 1976, there have been over 13,000 members join and enjoy OHG, the OHG International, Winter Park's Ski Meisters, and related senior skiing programs.

Bob Seibert

My experience with the OHG started in the summer of 1976 at the Pueblo Reservoir in Southern Colorado during the Hobie 16 Sailing Regatta.

That might seem a strange starting location for a story about thirty-plus years of great skiing, great friends, and great fun, but it is actually where it all started. It was there that I ran into, quite literally, Jay Abbott. Jay, along with Vino Anthony founded and ran the Copper Choppers program. It was through Jay, while waiting for the race committee meeting to determine who was at fault in the "collision at sea," that I found out about tryouts for the Copper Mountain Ski School.

After two attempts, and being glad I didn't make it the first year due to the snow drought of 1976, I was hired to teach and guide with the Copper Choppers. Little did I know back in December 1977 what a change that would make in my life!

With a little help—well actually a lot of help—from Jay, Mike Klysa, Dave Sanctuary, and numerous others, I finally, sort of, actually learned how to ski. At least, I learned enough to pass the Associates exam with what was then known as the Rocky Mountain Ski Instructor Association.

It was during that first year on Copper Mountain that I met three outstanding pioneers in the ski business: Tom Stein, Bill McGill, and Moe Mosley. They were just starting to hatch their idea for an adult ski group. What great insight!

It took me a few years to get old enough and wise enough to finally move over to the adult side of the Ski School and join the OHG staff. After teaching and guiding with the Choppers for more than ten years, I thought I was a slam dunk to get a position with the OHG. Little did I know that Mark "Sharky" Fish and Jim Lincoln were going to make me try out! After a day on the mountain, mainly doing demonstrations for the others who were trying out, I was offered a position as an OHG Guide. Let the fun begin!

When you ask around the Gang and the guides to discover what makes the group tick, you almost always hear about the positive energy, great attitudes, and all the fun that surrounds them. The OHG is an integration of the members, the mountain, and the guides. It is a unique mix that has lasted for more than thirty years and hopefully will last many, many more. I can hardly ever remember a grumpy member or guide. They just didn't last long.

I have skied all the faces on the front side of Union Bowl with silver haired grandmas, and spent just as enjoyable a day on the greens of Union Creek with those just getting back into the sport or slowing down as they face some of the challenges of age, each etching a memory that will last lifetime.

One of my more memorable experiences helped me see that the Gang was different. It happened in my first season, and we had just finished a warm up run. We headed off the top of E lift and were trying to decide where to head next. One lady, who was wearing a very nice one piece ski outfit, mentioned that she needed a comfort break. I said, "No problem, we can swing by Solitude and take a quick break." She replied, "No one waits for me," and promptly skied off into the trees! She emerged several minutes later, below the group and ready to go. Remember how I mentioned the one piece ski outfit? After that, I was ready for just about anything.

Each year, towards the beginning of the season, all the guides would spend a weekend in a clinic with the regular Ski School as a refresher on the mumbo-jumbo latest tech talk from PSIA. After a weekend of this I was riding up the chair with Stephan Jencsok discussing what we had just heard and how to apply it to our position as OHG Guides. It was then when we came up with the real, true job description of a OHG Guide: "making middle aged women smile." Quite frankly, we figured out our basic job was just that. What a gig! While somewhat facetious, it became the underlying principle that guided me on most of my guide days. This is supposed to be *fun!* Warren Miller once wrote something like, "It's not the number of runs or vertical feet that counts, it's the size of the smile on your face at the end of the day."

If you ever skied with me you have probably heard me tell you the simple truth that skis will not turn unless you have a smile on your face. I suggest that next time you're at the top of a hill, especially a more challenging one, you put a smile on your face and a song in your heart and dance down the mountain. The women would understand and the guys most often probably thought I was crazy. But I know that at the end of the day, "If Momma ain't happy, ain't nobody happy."

I miss the Gang, the Guides, and the Mountain. I hope one day soon to be once again smiling and singing my way down the slopes of Copper Mountain.

Thanks to all the wonderful people who make up the OHG. It is a synergy that is hard to beat. Many a mountain has tried but the true OHG will always be at Copper Mountain.

And, in closing, remember, "Speed is at the discretion of the user!" Be safe out there, have fun, and come back and do it another day.

Bob Seibert

Jim and Angie Leibold

In 1977, friends who were parishioners of Father Bill Magill told us about a ski club for older people (the minimum age then was 45) which was being started at Copper Mountain by three ski instructors. After a little investigation, we decided that the price was reasonable and we joined the groups at the very beginning of the Copper Mountain Over the Hill Gang Ski Team.

The opportunity to ski with people our own age and ability level enticed us into joining. Besides, we liked to ski at Copper, and had done so since it opened in 1972.

There are three vital aspects of the OHG: the opportunity to ski with people our own age and ability and enjoy group skiing; the opportunity to improve our ski technique by skiing with excellent ski instructors acting as our guides; and the opportunity to meet new people who are outdoor enthusiasts and have similar interests to ours.

One of our earliest memories is of Father Bill asking Angie and me to lead the first hike for OHG. He specified that he wanted it to be a true mountain climb. So for July 21, 1979, we chose Mt. Parnassus since it is a prominent peak as you drive eastbound out of the Eisenhower tunnel.

We heard lots of moans and groans from the members when we started, but most made it to the top. We were asked to lead easier hikes in the future and no more that were that difficult.

Angie and I also led the first highway clean-up on I-70. When we first did the clean-up, our stretch had never been cleaned and we soon ran out of bags!

On occasions when snow conditions and weather were not ideal for summer or winter activities, most members cheerfully accepted the fact that it was beyond our control and made the best of it. It was always inspiring to see how the members would be so positive in the face of challenges.

The OHG at Copper is the premier organization for people of similar age and ability to ski in groups and to enjoy other outdoor activities together. It is the leading organization that offers seniors the opportunity to improve ski technique by taking clinics and skiing each day with excellent, certified ski instructors.

As the number of senior skiers continues to increase, many more will benefit from the opportunities and experiences offered by the OHG.

Jim and Angie Leibold

Moe Dixon

I first encountered Copper Mountain in 1978 when I came to Colorado to ski. Although I have been involved in skiing and the entertainment world my whole life, we returned to Colorado and Copper Mountain in 1980 when I accepted a Ski School position; the best job I ever had. I was hired by Floyd Bashant to teach bumps and powder skiing at the "B" lift.

That was when I encountered the other "Moe" (Moe Mosley) (who, by the way, has a laugh that could start an avalanche). I've known him for over 30 years and he's one of the most positive individuals I've ever met. He is also truly one of the best instructors I ever knew or worked with. With him, it's always 100%. It was obvious that Bill Magill, Tom Stein, and Moe had a love for skiing, the Mountain, and the OHG Program.

In the early 80s, the OHG Program was operating on full throttle. In my first year with Copper Mountain Ski School, the OHG Ski Program was a stroke of luck. 1982 was the year the founders brought in 100 out-of-town skiers to the Mountain over three separate weeks from three different airlines each week to ski with the OHG. What a time we all had! The guests stayed near the "B" Lift. The snow was great, the bumps were right on, and a great time was had by all.

A few years later I moved over to coach ski racing at Ski Club Vail before returning to Copper.

The OHG creates magic every time their members step into their skis. I'm always honored and humbled by the fact that they ski all day and then come to hear my show

(where I perform at JJ's Tavern) and dance for 2½ hours.
How do they do it? They truly love to ski. And to live.

Moe Dixon, Musician, Skier

Sandy Shellworth Hildner

My earliest memory of the Over the Hill Gang was trying
out to be a guide in March of 1986 when Steve Olson was
the supervisor of the OHG. Wild Bill Kieser, an old friend
and star sailor, thought I would enjoy this group so I tried
out and discovered it was a very fun group.

Skiing and socializing with these energetic people was
so much fun! They also participated in so many other
sports and interests.

The vital aspects of the OHG are the interesting people, having fun skiing, and enjoying the outdoors. The
OHG gives members the ability to ski at their own levels,
to take clinics of their choice, and to be flexible with their
daily choice of group and the level at which they ski, with
or without their spouses. The greatest aspect is really
having *fun* with like-minded people.

After 21 years of guiding, I have so many inspiring
memories. One of my favorites is a day skiing with a
group when a blizzard suddenly blew in from Vail. My
group was starting down from the top of High Point.
Because these were whiteout conditions and it was very
windy and cold, we followed the chairs until we could go
into the woods on the left side of the Flyer. We paired up
and began singing very loudly (and badly) as we skied very
slowly through the trees. We were laughing very hard as
we sang. We were able to see better in the trees and made

our way down safely to the Easy Feeling run. Later, we all talked about how that was one of the best times and how it reminded us of when we were kids having fun.

Another time, I was giving a race clinic on the Master racers' race course (which was difficult). The group all went down the course at their own speed and did well. I found out after we were done that two of the guys who were having a great time were 83 years old! You could not tell their age by their skiing or level of enthusiasm.

The OHG is important because it gives older people an outlet for skiing with others when most people their age have quit skiing altogether. It is also an opportunity for socializing and having fun with other like-minded people and being able to have *fun* skiing with people of their own ability. It is also nice to have clinics available to help improve their skiing.

OHG helps keep older people active, healthy, and interacting with others who like to have fun. Even after some of these older people are injured, fellow members provide much needed support and encouragement to return to skiing.

OHG inspires people to want to come back by making it *fun* and flexible and asking them what they want, and delivering that!

I have retired from guiding, but I have enjoyed Copper Mountain's great skiing terrain and the high quality and friendship of its employees.

Sandy Shellworth Hildner

Mark "Sharky" Fish

In 1987, my wife and I relocated to Frisco, opening a little B&B and both taking jobs at Copper Mountain. I was hired by a guy named Shawn Smith (Smitty we called him), and little did I know that he would be teaching me, a fully certified instructor, how to ski. My first season passed quickly, as I recall, and I didn't hear much about the OHG. We all knew it existed, we knew a fellow instructor, Steve Olson, was running the show, and all was going well.

Then, as 1988 rolled around, Smitty asked me if I would be interested in going to a fall OHG party down in Denver. I thought to myself, "This is strange! Why would he want me to go to an old folks party?" But, I went.

We had a good time, met lots of great story tellers, and I didn't think much more about it. However, the next week, unbeknownst to me, I was selected by my fellow supervisors to become the new OHG supervisor. I was not a happy camper!

My disappointment didn't last long, and I was advised by a fellow supervisor, Don Coleman, who was deeply involved in the OHG for many years both before and after this time, that I should really consider taking the job.

So, I did. We hit the ground running, too. My job became a whole lot easier to understand with my first acquaintance, long time instructor and guide, Jim Lincoln. Jim took me under his wing and really helped me understand what needed to be done to keep this program rolling. I will always be indebted to him and his wise and experienced guidance.

Smitty was a busy guy and pretty much gave me free reign to do what I thought needed to be done, as long as I had the OK from the guy who ran the company, the CEO of Copper Mountain, Harry Mosgrove.

I was a nervous wreck the first time I was to report to Harry. Fortunately for me, he made me feel very welcome and was very anxious to get this program growing—and I do mean growing. When I asked him how large he would like to see the program become, he simply replied, "I'll let you know."

To grow like that, I was going to need help. Fortunately, we had another very important player working so hard behind the scenes, publishing the newsletter, keeping up with the fast growing membership, dealing with all the fun folks who wanted it and wanted it now. Thank you, Suzie Randolph!

I can remember my first meeting with the OHG Board of Directors and being told that they really didn't care to see the program become larger than 200 members. At this point in time, we had a group of about 100 members and 20 guides. Again, to my good fortune, one of my first confidants on the board was a guy named Howard Johnston. He worked very hard with me to convince the rest of the group that it might be good to get a little bit larger than 200 members.

The program was well supported by Copper and with 100 wonderful ambassadors, the word quickly got out that we were having a pretty special time at Copper Mountain. The first two years of my tenure, the group grew two fold and it became very apparent that I was greatly under-staffed—we needed more guides. We put together a hiring program with the help of Jim Lincoln and Dave "Petey" Peterson which really produced an outstanding guide staff. We pulled together a group of guides from all walks of life, mostly all professionals, many of whom were certified ski instructors. Talk about years of experience! These are the people that are truly responsible for the growth of the program.

I had no idea at the time how rewarding this position would become and how much it would affect my life. We continued to grow, and we outgrew the existing wine and cheese facility we had been using, and suddenly I was in the restaurant business. Many members and guides remember Jacque's Loft. Those were the days! Where else could you get exquisite cheese trays, hors d'oeuvres, all the pizza you could eat, $1 glasses of wine, all for the outrageous entry fee of $2.00. Those truly were the good old days, and boy did we have fun!

The outside activities grew as well. The groups put together hikes, bike rides, and ski trips, while the guides had a few fun trips of their own, including cat skiing at Monarch or Ski Cooper, or skiing the glades at Steamboat. They knew how to turn up the fun-dial to "high"! We also outgrew the locker room, and again the guides were so helpful, we put together a wonderful little facility they named the Shark's Den. Oh, by the way, I guess I should mention, Smitty nicknamed every supervisor, which is how my nickname "Sharkey" came to be. I was never certain why he picked that variety of fish, though. It certainly had nothing to do with my personality!

I would love to mention all of the guides, but that would be a book in itself. However, they were the greatest group of folks I have had the pleasure of knowing and working alongside. The guide staff the year I departed from Copper consisted of 120 guides and the membership had grown to about 1100.

We had a very happy family, the mountain was very satisfied with our growth, and we gained national recognition for our special OHG senior ski group.

I will close with this thought: with the boomers on the way, what a prime time to get this effort really going again! I want to thank Moe Mosley for all of his hard work and dedication to the group, not only as one of the founders, but as one of the best guides the program ever had.

All the best to everyone involved in this program.

Mark Fish

Ray Allen

Some years ago during the summer lull, I talked to Jim Olson, a friend and OHG guide, about going to work at Gold Peak at Vail. He looked at me and said, "You're too old to go to Gold Peak. You'd have a lot more fun working at Copper with the Over the Hill Gang." That started it all for me.

I thought my 25 years' experience teaching skiing, running a kids' program, being a ski school supervisor (and the weekend PR director) at Eldora gave me a lot of good experience. Because of that and my experience teaching adults at Loveland, I thought going to Copper and working with seniors would be rewarding.

I quickly learned that the three most vital aspects of OHG were the camaraderie, exercise, and commitment to skiing.

Some years ago, during an OHG lunch break, Mark "Sharkey" Fish introduced a group of 10th Mountain Division vets who immediately broke into a song they had sung while serving in the Division. The power of the history and their connection to one another, the mountains, and skiing was overwhelming.

OHG can be very important to the ski area, senior community, and guides. If the program is well managed, the members and guides will be great ambassadors for Copper. With guides that truly want to ski and enjoy their relationships with senior skiers, and remembering the three principles of guiding: safety first, having fun second, and teaching third, OHG will always be a success.

The future challenge for OHG will be to ensure that leadership continues to hire very experienced ski instructors who may no longer wish to work in ski school, yet still love the camaraderie of skiing with groups.

I really enjoyed guiding the OHG groups. I gave a lot to the program, but got a lot back.

Ray Allen

Kay and Neil Geitner

It was November 1997 at the Copper Mountain Ski School orientation when I was reacquainted with Sandy (Shellworth) Hildner. I had been hired to be an instructor in the kids' ski school Copper Choppers winter program, but she told me that I really needed to try out for and join the OHG ski group as a guide. I had not heard of the OHG at that time, but had known Sandy from about 1958 when we raced together in the Pacific Northwest. Based on her recommendation, I tried out with Sharkey (Mark Fish) and was hired. I decided to work in both programs for the 1987-88 season and make a decision at the end of the ski season as to which I preferred to pursue the following season. I chose the OHG and never looked back.

I think one of the most vital aspects of the OHG has always been the quality of the people involved, including both the members and the guides. It is a fabulous group of people who are passionate about skiing, the outdoors, and other sports. There is also an exceptionally high quality of skiing by members and guides, as well as emotional support for all participants. Everyone is involved in increasing their friendships and emotionally bolstering one another as we all enjoy one another's company. The overriding sense is one of *fun* with many skiing friends.

I make memories and am inspired by skiing with OHG members every day. Each day brings stories of inspiration and recovery from injuries (not all ski related) and illnesses, significant volunteer or paid work for the benefit of communities and individuals, and genuine care and support of each other. There is a huge volume of stories, events, and crazy, mixed up times. For example, the expansion of the "Women's Weekend" from a one-day ski clinic to a full weekend of activities beginning with a Friday night kick-off dinner, is a maze of fond memories of fun, crazy doings with lifelong women's friendships, and improved skiing to boot. It is where strangers became friends and supportive participants, and where connections were made for bike trips, travel, and all manner of meals and parties.

I think OHG is much more important than any member or guide has believed. It gives everyone a lift in the winter as you stay connected and vital with a group of people who are passionate about skiing with friends in the wonderful Colorado mountains. It is a reason to stay healthy, get in shape, and look *forward* to winter while many friends are moaning about the snowy months of winter and complaining about the snow and cold preventing them from doing what they want to do.

The connections with friends, members, and guides are a reason for personal growth and well-being. A void is created in our lives when we don't have this kind of connection to a group such as the OHG.

The current and future importance of the OHG will depend on the continuation of gathering and connecting people who are passionate about skiing with friends, across different, varying skill levels. Presenting a safe, fun, and supportive environment for people in the winter to meet, ski, and enjoy themselves is the essence of the OHG. Copper Mountain should make it as easy as possible for the growing number of senior skiers who are "coming of age" to continue to ski with new and old friends. The fun and group camaraderie is a great benefit, after all, for those who do not like to ski alone for a day, let alone the whole winter! Many friends from outside of Colorado stop skiing when their buddies stop, or think of themselves as being too old to continue. OHG shows everyone how to continue to age with skiing and friends in a supportive and fun group.

The emotional intangibles of the club can be difficult to understand from outside, but it is where the club and mountain earn a supportive and loyal base of skiers who will champion Copper Mountain to their friends and families. For this, and many other reasons, OHG should continue growing the membership and the quality and capabilities of the Guides into the future.

Kay and Neil Geitner

Paul Kresge

In the late 80s and early 90s while skiing Copper with my close friend Bill Kieser, I was introduced to the OHG. Bill was a "follow me" kind of guy, and encouraged me to join in the groups he was skiing with. It was a great crowd then with some very top notch guides like Sandy Hildner, Tom Bradley (Bradley's Plunge), Jacque deLormie, Steve Combs, and others.

In 1993, Bill encouraged me to try out as a guide. Sharkey and his hiring team put us through some paces, and I did not make it until a 2nd tryout a year later. That was the first year that they lifted the membership cap and added Tuesdays as one of the organized ski days. There were a record 26 guides that joined the Guide crew that season. Only a few from that recruiting class are left. We had a great run with mountain improvements and the après ski sessions in Jacques's Loft in the old Clock Tower building.

Skiing with the gang then was the best, although Sharkey and his sidekick Jim Lincoln ruled with an iron fist. We'd have lunch in Solitude Station and had Irish coffee pouring for the group. If I came in late for lunch, Sharkey would pull me aside and chew me out.

The Gang has always been a generous and caring group, giving freely to the local charities, and Doris's mitten tree at Christmas was one of the big hits.

During the course of its existence, the OHG program has become the première program for skiers over 50. The most important aspect of the program now is the continuing full support and encouragement from top Copper Mountain and POWDR management team members. With a very dedicated management team and a very experienced guide staff assisting the members on the hill, the program will continue to be popular. Copper will need to find the delicate balance between value and pricing to continue growing the program.

I'm fortunate to get to ski with the Gang well over 20 days out of each season. Each day is a special day! The days start with jovial camaraderie and banter with the guide staff which then carries over to the meeting area and the group splits. Over the years I have made some lifelong friends and I truly enjoy working the crowd. I get to ski at the top levels of the groups, and we have enjoyed some outstanding powder days, and I have often arranged some special cat trips to Tucker Mountain, as well.

The most rewarding aspect of the Gang is seeing the continual improvement in the members' skiing confidence throughout the season. For many, this confidence translates into better technique and skiing skill-sets. The best part is exploring the hard to find areas of Copper and seeking out the really good snow, then seeing the big smiles on the faces of the members during the experience and after a very satisfying day.

The Gang is still a very vital part of the industry and

the health of Copper Mountain. It may not be a gold mine in direct revenue for the Mountain, but the goodwill and industry-setting standards it establishes will continue to keep Copper a premiere place for the Front Range and destination skier. Copper also gains a huge ripple from friends and family purchasing real estate at the base area and around the region, skiing with the Gang, and otherwise skiing and spending at Copper because of the Gang.

The future of the sport is still with the skier. New equipment is allowing many older enthusiasts to return to the sport. Ski schools are still 65% skier with the balance snowboard and other sports. Park & pipe and off-piste experiences are becoming more popular, too. There is discretionary income to be used and as long as the Gang is there to provide a spot for the groups to gather and have guided and coached skiing, then the program will flourish. In addition, Copper Mountain needs to cross-market between the Youth Ski and Ride School and the OHG to provide some synergy between parents and OHG members and offer some sort of package-deal or slight discounts for members that have kids in Copper's Ski and Ride School and ski with the Gang. Youth taking lessons while the parents are enjoying a day of guided skiing and coaching offers an ideal opportunity.

Copper needs to fully embrace the Gang and take advantage of the wide demographics and economics the membership offers.

With the full support of the management team this program will maintain as the premiere senior ski program for the nation.

Paul Kresge

Sally Brand

When my family moved to Colorado in 1990 and winter arrived, I immediately headed to the ski slopes. Our daughter was on the ski patrol at Copper Mountain, so it was a given I would ski at Copper.

I had skied some in the mid-west, mostly on little hills made from landfills, and had spent one week at Breckenridge in 1979. My only other ski experience prior to that had been in 1962 when I spent a week at Loveland staying with college friends at the home of a ski instructor. During that trip, I was given wooden skis and leather boots as my rental equipment, along with a week's worth of lessons.

My first winter at Copper was spent at Union Creek. I didn't have lessons, just fun days on the mountain on my own. The next year, my sister was living in Colorado and she encouraged me to try the middle of the mountain. My daughter also mentioned the Over the Hill Gang and their presence on the mountain, but I was only 48, and too young to join. One day I met some of the OHG members at Solitude Station and they told me to get on the waiting list because it took two years to get in. This was perfect, since I would turn 50 in December two years later. I think I joined the Gang one day after my 50th birthday.

I started slow, in the No Worries group, and skied often with Moe Mosley and Jim Leibold. They were so patient, and their knowledge of the mountain and the stories they told made the experience exhilarating. My first winter with the Gang, I skied about 30 days while working full time in Denver. As my skiing improved, so did the number of days I skied each winter. I never got past the Decline group, but I learned to ski trees, bumps, and steeps. My favorite ski days were those with a little powder up top on Retreat, Gold Digger, and in Hallelujah Bowl. My ability to ski such places was totally due to the guidance of the OHG guides. They took me from a rank beginner who was not in great physical shape to one who enjoyed the steep and deep.

Because I learned so much about the mountain and had heard many stories about Copper from OHG guides, I became an Ambassador and enjoyed four years of service greeting guests and leading tours of the mountain. Those were the years I skied 40 to 50 days per season while still being active in OHG and also working and traveling for my job.

Beyond the great ski days, I was asked to serve on the Social Committee in 1998. We had fun parties that were always well-attended. Eventually I served on the OHG Board and in 2003 I became President (chairperson) of the Board. That was the year we celebrated the 25th anniversary of the signing of the OHG Charter with a big party at Copper. We were privileged to have many charter members there along with OHG International board members. Our keynote speaker was Moe Mosley. He gave a wonderful overview of the history of the Gang and the history of Copper, as well. This was probably my favorite time with OHG as I was able to become immersed in the history of the mountain.

I feel that the Gang is very important to the older generation. Skiing is such a good physical sport, and the social interaction that the Gang provides with others of like interests has been the beginning of many friendships—and some marriages, as well.

I hope the future of the Gang remains bright because it is truly a unique group that offers so much to the aging skier population.

Sally Brand

Harley Van De Wege

I started skiing in 1961 with a ½ day lesson at Ski Idlewild, between Winter Park and Sol Vista ski areas.

My lovely wife, Maureen, and I joined the Over the Hill Gang International in 1990 to help reduce the cost of skiing. However, their lift ticket rate reduction was not too substantial so we did not end up using it much.

Around 1992 we decided we would like to become better skiers and decided to take some lessons at Copper Mountain. At the time, they had an early season package that was 4 days over 2 weekends in early December so we signed up for them 2 seasons in a row. I had received no other lessons beside the ½ day at Ski Idlewild and now describe my skiing at that time as being a "terminal intermediate."

We were skiing one day at Copper in 1994, the year we moved to Summit County full time, and went into Solitude Station for an early lunch. We saw a group of older skiers on the upper level who were obviously having a great time. We asked one of them what the group was and they told us they were the OHG. We asked if our OHGI membership was the same thing and were told it was not, and that this group was unique to Copper Mountain. The person we talked to did invite us to have lunch with them but we declined. We researched the program and were told there was a waiting list, but we decided to get on it, anyway. We were able to join for the 95-96 season and started skiing with the group that winter.

After some years skiing with the Gang, I tried out 2 times to be a Guide under Mark "Sharky" Fish and 2 times under Mark Gidney before I was hired at last. I think that there must have been some unwritten mercy rule that if you try out 4 times you have to be hired! So in February of 1997 I was hired as a Guide and continued to guide through 2009-2010 season.

The Copper OHG members and their volunteer leadership are some of the most interesting, active, friendly people I have ever met. They come from all walks of life and most have very unique and interesting backgrounds with the related life stories to tell. It was a distinct pleasure to get to know the people in this group and I have made many good friends and ski partners from my time with the OHG. This ski group attracts and fosters people with the conviction that as we grow old we can still have a very healthy mind, body, and spirit.

The crowning experience of my Copper OHG career was my association with the guide staff. I have never worked with a group that was more dedicated to providing an exceptional, positive experience for their customers, the skiing members. There may have been a guide here or there that guided for purely selfish reasons, but they didn't last very long. Most were more interested in the kind of ski day the members were having than in their own ski day, and that is as it should be.

At the time I was a guide, Copper Mountain was extremely supportive of the Copper OHG program, especially in the training the guides had available to them. Joe Quarantillo (a ski school instructor and supervisor at the Copper Ski and Ride School) was very instrumental in a great deal of this support and provided an open and progressive atmosphere for the program. About 1/3 of the guide staff of 90 was certified ski instructors and taught regular ski school classes when the School needed the help. Copper trainers were always available and ready to help all the guides in developing both their skiing and teaching skills. I progressed from the "terminal intermediate" I was when I joined as an OHG member to a Level 2 Certified alpine ski instructor, mostly under the tutelage of Jeff (Stumpy) Stump. Many of the guide staff and some of the other ski instructors have become very close friends and life-long ski companions for me. Several have been very positive influences in my life and have been people that I look up to for their hard work, honesty, and integrity. Jim Leibold has been my mentor throughout my time at Copper Mountain, and the epitome of a lifelong skier.

The Copper Mountain program was very instrumental in making me a better skier and a better ski instructor. Unfortunately, in my zeal, I sometimes overwhelmed my wife Maureen with my new found tips, techniques, and exercises. But in the long run she became a much better skier too, and now skiing is a big part of both of our lives.

The Copper Mountain program was such a beneficial influence on my skiing that my goal became to leave the program in better shape than when I started with it in 1995. I feel in the 12 years I was a guide, the total scope of the program increased progressively through expanded content and the number of clinics available for members, improvement in the guide selection, and improved talent and skiing knowledge of the guide staff. This was not unique to the years I was guiding as the same progression had taken place since the inception of the Copper OHG. My many thanks to the many people involved for allowing me to have enjoyed this opportunity.

Harley Van De Wege

Stew and Linda Everard

(Stew was President of the OHG for many years, and was a principal player in maintaining the OHG during some of the program's greatest challenges during the summer of 2010. If it wasn't for Stew's efforts, the OHG would very likely have ceased to be, once again demonstrating the intensity and passion of the OHG members.)

In 1994, I had retired after 31 years in a major technology company and started a new career extension as a consultant. My first major consulting engagement was going to have me in the Denver and Colorado Springs area for a couple of years. Since we had always skied in New England with an occasional trip to Colorado, Salt Lake City or Jackson Hole, my wife Linda and I decided that we would rent a condo in the Colorado mountains and try skiing out in that part of the world for a season. We rented a condo and moved to Breckenridge in June 1994. We quickly found out that Summit County was a truly unique part of the world and had spectacular weather during the summer.

One evening, while having dinner at the Ski Tip Lodge in Keystone, we happened to strike up a conversation with Bill and Dee Simon. During the conversation, they recommended that we join the Over the Hill Gang at Copper. We filed that information away and promptly forgot about it.

Winter arrived early and the skiing was fantastic from November 1st right through Christmas. We were thinking, "Wow! What a place this is!"

We mainly skied Breckenridge and Keystone with an occasional trip to Copper. Another friend of mine, John Reid, had retired and purchased a place in Frisco. The three of us were retired ski bums.

In December 1994, we remembered the Simons' recommendation of the OHG and decided to see what it was all about. Off we went to Copper Mountain to join the OHG for a day. I can't remember how we joined up with the OHG that first day, but we quickly decided that the OHG was for us. Like many a husband and wife, we ski at different levels and this was wonderful for Linda to finally have people to ski with of the same ability instead of trying to keep up with me or our kids. At that time, new members were given red name tags to identify them as first year members. The older members really went out of their way to make us feel at home. Our first exposure to wine & cheese was in the old clock tower in Center Village. What a pleasant surprise that was! We paid a dollar, the guides served the beer and wine, and the appetizers were awesome. Wine and Cheese became the evening meal for many an OHG member.

As typically happens, the new kids on the block often

skied together in the same OHG group. For us, it was Jim Novak, Rich Seal, Lee Vorble, John Reid, and me. Other than Lee, we were all intermediate skiers that first season. What a difference a year makes! By skiing in a group and being encouraged by the guides, there was a dramatic improvement in our skiing that first year. Then, we started to meet new friends and began a social life that was beyond our wildest dreams. Without joining the OHG, we probably would have rented the condo in Breckenridge for one season and then moved back to New England. However, year one was a huge success, and we decided to stay for another year. We rented the same condo in Breckenridge, again.

Stew & Linda Everard

Jack and Sharon Godwin

Many years ago, now, after accepting a transfer to Columbus, Ohio, it became obvious to me that, to survive the winters, I would be forced to deal with the snow and ice. So, at age 50, I put on my first ski boots and skis and set out to tackle the sheet ice, "Devil's apples," and "corn snow" of the mid-west and north-east. At the end of the season, I was managing almost any trail with jerky "Z" turns. I was not skiing. I was just surviving.

Fast forward to 1999 when I moved to Florida and linked up with four guys who went to Summit County for a week each year. They invited me to join them, and I did. Each year we skied Breckenridge, Keystone, Vail, and Cooper Mountain. In 2006, we met Su Allen at JJ's Tavern while she was the President of the Over the Hill Gang.

She introduced us to a few of the members and invited us to try the OHG. At that time guests could ski free with OHG once and pay $50 to ski with the Gang for a week. We tried a day and were immediately taken by the professionalism (and tolerance) of the guides and the friendliness of the members. From this one encounter, I went from a 6-day-a-year skier to 40 days a year and bought a condo in Silverthorne (from Joanne, an OHG guide).

Over the next several years the OHG experience was phenomenal. Thanks to guides like Moe Mosley, I was taught to ski and not just survive. I no longer had to work at making "Zs" down the mountain, but rather learned to make controlled, rounded, graceful turns. Without going into the details, one guide named Steve Hultquist gave me a few tips that were so profound I actually had an epiphany that created a step-change in my ability.

Aside from the technical end of skiing, the guides added another dimension to the experience. For example, I remember Stephan Jencsok talking about the Hungarian Rebellion and taking us to his "special place" on the mountain to see the dark, dark blue of the sky. And Jim Leibold who always had treats for us at the end of the day.

My wife, Sharon, also had several positive experiences she remembers well. For years, she had consistent problems turning left. During one OHG day, her Guide inspected her boots and posture and determined that she had a severe cant problem. After a shim was placed in her boot, the problem was corrected and as a result, she can now make proper turns in both directions. Another time she was standing with her group mid-mountain, slipped on ice, and broke a bone in her shoulder. The guide gave her attention, turned the group over to another guide, and escorted her down the mountain, staying with her until satisfied that she was in good hands.

The OHG was good to me. The guides were generous with their offerings. I have made lasting friendships with many of the members, including Su, Joanne, Katherine and Jack, Tom and Bonnie, Cloud (Claudia Stein), Ed, Sophia, Stewart, Caroline, and a list too long to write.

Jack and Sharon Godwin

Claudia Stein

My earliest involvement with the OHG is what I believe "saved my life" after 41 years of marriage and becoming a widow. At the time (2006), I was employed at Copper Mountain in the ticket office. While riding the Summit Stage to work one morning, I happened to sit next to an OHG guide who engaged me in conversation. I told the guide that I didn't think I would ever want to ski again since I had lost my skiing partner. The guide told me about an upcoming clinic sponsored by OHG which might help me. The clinic was entitled: "Stress-free skiing." I still have the letter I was asked to write to myself during that session:

Dear Claudia,

When you went to the ski clinic, you were looking for a way to gain encouragement to continue skiing without your husband. I think you accomplished this. You found that skiing with others who are also trying to continue on in the sport and improve their skills, can be "safe" and "fun." If you keep on skiing, you will enjoy it, you will improve and you will be able to ski with your grandchildren. Once again, you were reminded that ACTION is created by thought, and POSITIVE thinking creates POSITIVE action. Soooooo get the ANTS out of your pants and replace them with PATS.

Love, Claudia

ANTS = AUTOMATIC NEGATIVE THOUGHTS
PATS = POSITIVE AUTOMATIC THOUGHTS

After that clinic, I was sold on continuing to ski and the OHG, and I have been a member for the past 6 years. Not only do I *love* skiing now, but I have never skied better. The guides have taught me everything I know and I am able to (almost) keep up with my grandchildren. I am forever grateful for the Over the Hill Gang at Copper Mountain.

It is *vital* that seniors who love to ski, have a *safe environment* in which to continue to pursue their love of the sport no matter what their age. The oldest person I have skied with in the group is 84. What a role model!

It is *vital* that seniors continue to enjoy and have FUN while skiing, and the OHG definitely provides such an atmosphere.

It is *vital* that the paying members of OHG feel *respected* and *included* when decisions are made to change policies which affect them. This is the single most important thing which will encourage new membership and retain current members.

I am indebted to the OHG for making my life as a widow manageable. I now *live* to ski in the winter and I have met so many wonderful people with whom I can "play" year 'round in Summit County and never feel lonely. My daughter and two grandchildren now live nearby and will also be "playing" at Copper Mountain, learning to love it as much as I do. I hope the leadership will find a way to document the kind of monetary support OHG seniors contribute to the mountain while entertaining family and friends. We spend large amounts on tickets, lodging, lessons, equipment, entertainment and food in addition to our season's pass and OHG fees.

Claudia Stein

Bill and Janis Erdkamp

Janis and I were so appreciative of the Over the Hill Gang. It was the best thing that we have ever done. I want to share with you an experience that tops everything:

On March 9th 2010, we met a man named Steve on the bus from Frisco who was somewhat handicapped. He had yet to get the needed knee replacements to correct the issues. At the time, Steve taught at Loyola in Chicago and was on spring break. He agreed when Janis and I invited him to be our guests for a guided OHG day of skiing the next day.

As we met him at the bus the next morning, he promptly slipped on the ice and ended up on his backside. Although a little sore from the fall, he decided to join us in a "No Worries Mate" group with Moe in the lead and Willis as the tail guide. Steve started out really struggling to get down the green slopes and at one point crashed into me. Willis and I got him back on his skis and up the lift we went again. Then Moe, with his "Yabadaba-doo" and gentle encouragement, started working with Steve and transformed his skiing before our eyes. Before it was even time to go into lunch, I was astounded at how well he skied. Cloud Stein then invited Steve to the Après Ski that afternoon, which included the OHG World Racing Championships awards ceremony. Steve was welcomed by all the members, and he decided to join the OHG. Then, to top off everything, he medaled in the ceremonies for having the Biggest Feet!

We had decided to join when the homebuilding industry went through a slow period, and had the best ski season that winter making new friends and learning to ski better.

Thanks to all in the OHG.

Bill and Janis Erdkamp

The Gold Run Award

During the 2004–2005 season Chuck Armstrong gave Joe Quarantillo, the OHG supervisor at the time, a pair of old skis that Chuck thought Joe might be able to use for the Copper OHG. The skis had belonged to Chuck's paternal uncle, Archie, and were Northland skis from the mid- to late-1920's.

Joe wisely decided to award one of the skis each year to the outstanding female and the other to the outstanding male OHG Guide. For the first award, at the banquet at the end of the 2005–2006 season, he selected Kay Geitner and Tom Snow to be the recipients. During the 2007–2008 season the skis were professionally restored, since they had been in a flooded basement for a time.

The skis were awarded through the 2010 season, for 5 seasons, presented each season to two outstanding guides for their contribution to the Copper OHG program:

| 2006 | Kay Geitner | Tom Snow |
| 2007 | Jennifer Walker | Harley Van De Wege |

2008	Winnie Johnson	Moe Mosley
2009	Kay Geitner	Paul Kresge
2010	Sara Swain	Pete Sowinski

Senior Skiing Across the Ski Industry

Those who have participated in winter sports for three, four, or even five decades may remember those earlier years of pulling into a ski area and looking for a parking space as close as possible to the lift up the mountain.

The parking lot was not marked or even plowed. It may have been full of fresh powder snow midwinter, or have been icy in the springtime. You might find that the mud could cover the sole of your ski boot up to the boot laces or even higher.

As you gathered your ski gear, you could only hope that the old car engine used for the lift would have enough gas and power to pull the skiers up the hill on the rope tow or T-bar. If not, hiking up the mountain to ski down was your only option. It was still skiing, but the extra work often shortened the ski day considerably!

In those early years, developers and engineers worldwide, through sometimes Herculean efforts, never gave up in their quest to provide great mountain experiences for the winter sport enthusiast. These years have been a journey, and there are many people that are unknown and unmentioned who have made skiing what it is today. Every skier and snowboarder owes a debt of gratitude to those who created the experience we now enjoy.

Today, many professional associations are intertwined together to benefit the winter sport industry as a whole.

National Ski Area Association

The National Ski Areas Association (NSAA) was established in 1962 and was headquartered in New York, NY. In 1989 NSAA merged with SIA (Snowsports Industries America) and moved to McLean, VA. The merger was dissolved in 1992 and NSAA was relocated to Lakewood, CO. Because of its central geographic location, NSAA is located in the same office building as the Professional Ski Instructors of America, the National Ski Patrol and the regional office of the 10th Mountain Division in a suburb west of Denver.

The NSAA's primary objective is to meet the needs of ski area owners and operators nationwide and to foster, stimulate, and promote growth in the industry. They represent more than 313 alpine resorts that account for more than 90% of the skier and snowboarder visits nationwide. There are more than 414 supplier members who provide equipment, goods, and services to the mountain resort industry.

NSAA performs additional services to the ski industry

such as analyzing and distributing ski industry statistics, providing conferences and trade shows, publishing industry publications, being active in state and federal government affairs, publishing employee training materials on industry issues of State and Federal Compliance Regulations, environmental laws, aerial tramway safety, resort operations, and guest services.

In addition, their publications to the membership include subjects like safety, risk management, tree-well and deep-snow safety, kids on lifts, general resort concerns, the skier/snowboarder responsibility code, sun safety on the slopes, general safety facts and tips, ski area vehicle maintenance, trail signage, environmental concerns and recommendations, accounts/database management, climate change, and more.

They also collaborate closely with two other key snowsports organizations:

- The PSIA/AASI, and
- The National Ski Patrol

The PSIA/AASI

The Professional Ski Instructors of America/American Association of Snowboard Instructors is the national organization for snowsports instruction in the United States.

There are nine Regional Divisions, each of which were originally founded and operated independently, setting up their own rules, regulations, and training programs. For example, the Eastern Division was operating in the 1930s, the Rocky Mountain Division in the 1950s, and so on across the country.

Initially there were no universal standards for teaching skiing, or later snowboarding. Instructors could choose to teach Austrian, French, or Swiss methods, to name just a few of the more popular options. That situation, plus the fact that the instructor certification standards were so different from one part of the country to another, led to the formation of a national organization for ski instruction—the PSIA. While the Divisions are still independent, their integration through the PSIA national organization provides consistency and collaboration across the country.

PSIA History

With a goal of establishing and promoting standards for how skiing was taught in the United States, PSIA was incorporated in the fall of 1961 by a group of seven committed instructors: Bill Lash, Jimmy Johnston, Paul Valar, Doug Pfeiffer, Don Rhinehart, Max Dercum, and Curt Chase.

By 1964, a truly American ski technique had taken shape, described in PSIA's first manual, The Official American Ski Technique. The American Ski Technique evolved into the American Teaching Method and eventually to what is now called the American Teaching System (ATS). The ATS was unique in its focus on skills rather than forms, contributing to the approach used with senior skiers, who often experience a range of both temporary and permanent limitations.

With the growing popularity of snowboarding in the 1980's, PSIA saw the need to do for snowboard instruction what it had done for ski instruction, and thus began developing snowboard instruction material. The first training and education programs were developed in 1987, and in 1989 the association published its first snowboard-oriented education resource, the Snowboard Instruction Manual.

Embracing the full scope of how snowboarding fit within its educational tenets, PSIA formed AASI in 1997. Fully committed to sharing the passion of the skiing and riding experience, the organization is now known as PSIA/AASI.

PSIA/AASI supports area management through research and development of instructional programs in:

- Alpine Skiing
- Snowboarding
- Nordic Skiing
- Adaptive Skiing and Snowboarding for those with special needs and limitations

The association also develops educational materials and programs to serve specific ski and snowboard demographics, such as children's instruction and freestyle specializations.

PSIA/AASI's national office is in Lakewood, Colorado, and there are nine regional divisions across the country:

- Alaska
- Central
- Eastern
- Intermountain
- Northern Intermountain
- Northern Rocky Mountain
- Northwest

- Rocky Mountain
- Western

The divisions provide services to the members in their specific part of the country and support their local members through education, certification, and PSIA/AASI membership services. In addition, PSIA/AASI represents the United States to the rest of the world through the International Ski Instructors Association.

Over the years, the majority of Copper Mountain OHG guides have been certified PSIA/AASI instructors, including at times both telemark and snowboard certifications.

National Ski Patrol (NSP)

Another important program for the skiing and snowboarding public to know and appreciate is the National Ski Patrol (NSP), the national organization of volunteer and professional ski patrollers.

In March 1938, while he was officiating the National Downhill ski race at Mount Mansfield in Stowe, VT., Roger F. Langley, then president of the National Ski Association, had an industry-changing idea. Langley was impressed by the "super patrol" for the race that Charles Minot "Minnie" Dole had created from members of the Mt. Mansfield, Pittsfield, and Burlington patrols. While watching the race at Shambles Corners on the Nosedive trail, Langley asked Dole if he would organize a national patrol like the one in use at the race. Not one to shy away from a challenge, and having lost a friend on the slopes two years earlier, "Minnie" accepted, and the National Ski Patrol was born.

Today, the nonprofit National Ski Patrol still adheres to the creed of "Service and Safety" established more than 70 years ago. As the industry has evolved, so too has the NSP. The emergence of new snowsports like snowboarding, tubing, snow-biking, and snow-skating has introduced new equipment and terrain, requiring new safety and rescue techniques and emergency care methods to be developed and taught. In addition, the emergence of so-called "extreme skiing" through the wider distribution of ski movies and greater access to the backcountry has brought new training and regimen requirements for NSP members.

As the leading authority for on-mountain safety, the NSP is dedicated to serving the public and outdoor recreation industry by providing education and accreditation to emergency care and safety service providers.

The organization comprises more than 28,000 members servicing over 650 patrols, including alpine, Nordic, and auxiliary patrollers. Their members work on behalf of local ski and snowboard areas to improve the overall experience for the public enjoying the wintertime great outdoors.

NSP Programs

The men and women of the NSP are great friends to the skiing and riding customers and, on occasion, the backcountry skiers that sometimes pose a safety problem to themselves or their party. Some of the programs of learning and assistance are:

- Training of Mountain Hosts
- Outdoor Emergency Care

- Mountain Travel & Rescue
- Safety Team Training
- Avalanche Safety and Rescue
- Training of Young Adults in Safety to be part of NSP
- Training Seniors on Safety
- Nordic Safety Training
- Development of Their Own Patrol
- NSP Certification
- Training of Women NSP
- Telecommunications
- Transportation of the Injured
- Creating and Providing Training videos
- Facts about Slope and Helmet Use
- Chairlift Safety for Adults and Children

The NSP represents the best of passionate snowsports participants, giving of themselves in order to share the sport safely with others, introducing them to the beauty, power, and transformational experiences available sliding down a mountain on snow.

The **OHG** was fortunate to have Hart Axley, a member of the Colorado Ski Hall of fame who assisted greatly with both the Rocky Mountain and The National Ski Patrol, and donated many, many hours to their wonderful yearly agendas, involved with the program.

A Copper Mountain OHG Chronology

1969

On August 12, 1969, a "study permit" was issued by the Forest Service for approximately 2,500 acres of future ski trails in the Arapahoe National Forest (Copper Mountain area).

Records show that Chuck Lewis may also have been in the business circle of Copper Mountain at the time.

Thus, Copper Mountain was born of a master plan which was unique both in depth and detail.

1971

Prior to the beginning of construction in 1971, the developers spent 2½ years studying every aspect of the project, including financing a great number of area studies critical to creating a total recreational resort.

Copper receives US Forest Service Permit. Trail and

lift construction begins. Zoning approved by the Board of County Commissioners.

Many months of construction would follow before the resort opened.

1972

On December 5, 1972, Copper Mountain Resort opened for visitors with six new buildings, and 20 trails with a combined length of 14 miles, on 290 acres accessed by five lifts.

Lift ticket prices were $7.50 per day, and increased to $9 later that season.

Lifts B, C, E, F and G and two buildings (The Center and Solitude) open. Copper's offices were located on the third floor of the Center Building. Copper Junction, Summit House, Ten Mile Haus, and Timber Creek were constructed.

1973

Installed I and B-1 Lifts. Buildings constructed: Anaconda, Copper Valley, Peregrine, Snowflake, Snowbridge Square, Summit House East, Wheeler House and Village Point.

The dedication ceremonies were held on February 23, 1973.

1975

Installed Mitey Mite Beginners Lift.

1976-1977

Installed H Lift. Buildings constructed: Togwotee and Copper Mountain Inn.

The OHG pilot program zm was developed (18 started and by the end of the ski year there were 25).

Installed J Lift, double chair.

1976 World Cup held at Copper Mountain, resulting in renaming of Trail #8 to Rosi's Run in honor of Rosie Mittermaire of West Germany who won the World Cup that year on that run.

Members of the OHG Pilot Program worked the World Cup races.

1977-1978

Development of OHG with the charter stating, "The purpose of the organization is to promote physical and mental health of members over the age of 45 by providing skiing, social and fraternal activities." After the first 18 months, this was amended to age 50.

Formal legal formation of the OHG as a non-profit corporation.

1979

Opened half of the East (Alpine) parking lot, Transportation Center building, and A, C-1 chairlifts. The Lodge at Copper Mountain, Foxpine Inn, Bridge End were built. Club Med was under construction.

1980

Apex Oil purchases Copper Mountain Resort. The new owners were Sam Goldstein and Paul "Tony" Novelly. Village Shuttle Road paved from East lots to West Lake. Mountain Plaza and Club Med construction was completed.

1981

Union Creek Base Lodge and K and L Lifts are built. T surface lift was also installed. West Lake Lodge, Beeler

Place Townhomes were constructed.

The Over the Hill Gang International, Inc. was chartered on December 18, 1981 at Copper Mountain by three PSIA part-time ski instructors. Copper Mountain was not part of the venture.

A gala benefit for Colorado Ski Museum was held on 10/23/1981.

OHG entered a joint venture with United, Frontier and Continental Airlines and travel agencies to bring 100 skiers to Colorado on each flight. Dates of the trip were:

- January 18-25, 1982,
- February 1-8, 1982, and
- March 29-April 5, 1982

1982

West Lake Lodge was completed and the Shuttle Road paved from East lots to Beeler Place. Easy terrain of Union Bowl opens with R-lift. Buildings constructed: Spruce Lodge and Village Square.

Moe Mosley donated his 1/3 interest in both organizations (OHG Copper Mountain and OHG International) to the other two founders to assist them. He continued instructing and guiding at Cooper Mountain.

A group of OHG skiers migrated back to Winter Park.

Pope John XXIII became an Honorary Member. Letter sent by Bill & Tom who received a letter in response from Pope John.

1983

B lift Clubhouse opens with food, restrooms, and skier services. S lift opens expert skiing in Union Bowl. Village

Square East and West and Conference Center opens. Spruce Lodge was completed.

In 1983 Magill and Stein swapped the remaining shares in each other's organizations and became separate owners, with Father Bill owning OHG Copper Mountain and Tom owning the OHGI.

1984

E lift is reconstructed increasing capacity. Copper Mountain Athletic Club opens.

President Ford became an Honorary Member of both OHG organizations.

1985

Spaulding Bowl opens with A-1 and Storm King lifts. Telemark Lodge is completed. Golf Course is redeveloped to a 7,000 yard par 70 championship course designed by Pete & Perry Dye.

Tom Stein sold the OHGI with about 2,000 members.

Bill Magill retired and moved to Florida.

1986

American Flyer lift opens as Copper Mountain's first high speed "detachable" quad. The Greens at Copper Mountain opens and phase 1 of The Woods at Copper Creek.

Bill Magill sold the Copper Mountain OHG to Copper Mountain and the OHG Advisory Board of Members was formed by Harry Mosgrove. The position of OHG Supervisor was created within the Copper Mountain Ski and Ride School.

Prior to the sale of the OHG in 1986, no financial assistance was ever given to the OHG organization.

Harry Mosgrove opened the waiting list over the 1987-88 season, there were 1200 members plus 352 on the waiting list.

1987

Phase II of The Woods at Copper Creek is completed.

1989

American Eagle lift opens providing two high speed quads from the base area.

1992

When the Climax Mine closed, the Climax Co. offered the reservoir for sale. Harry Mosgrove, President of Copper Mountain put together a group including Keystone Resort, Summit County Government, and Copper Mountain to purchase the Clinton Ditch and Reservoir Co. The sale completed on August 25, 1992 and was a great move for all.

The next time you drive up Fremont Pass, look at the large reservoir on the left just as you reach the top of the Pass. It is pristine.

1994

Copper Bowl opens adding approx. 250 acres of expert, high Alpine terrain to Copper's offerings. Timberline Express lift installed.

OHG's 1st Women's Ski Clinic March 6, 1994 with 40 women members and 6 women guides.

1995

Mountain Chief lift installed.

British Columbia-based Intrawest Corp. partners with Ralcorp Holdings to develop a $400 million village at Ralcorp's Keystone Ski Area which was named "River Run".

1996

Intrawest buys Canada's Whistler Ski Area and Copper Mountain for $192 million.

Blackjack lift installed in Copper Bowl.

1997

Stinger lift installed.

1998

Intrawest launches Phase I of the resort's multi-year renaissance by breaking ground in the Village. Copper Mountain opens the Super Bee lift, Colorado's first six-passenger, high speed detachable lift. Copper also makes significant snowmaking improvements in addition to opening Excelerator lift, Copper Station, and Copper Springs Lodge. Glide Magic Carpet lift installed. Eldon Beck sketches the initial plan for the Village at Copper focusing on the pedestrian usage and flows.

1999

Groundbreaking marked the beginning of a new era for Copper Mountain, solidifying the launch of Phase II of the resort's multi-year $500 million renaissance. The Schoolhouse at Union Creek opens offering a "kids only" building for Ski School.

2000

Installed Rug Rat and Easy Rider Magic Carpets.

2001

Intrawest joins with owners of Aspen Skiing Co. to develop a $400 million village at Snowmass Ski Area. Five years later, the companies sell the project to California developer WestPac Investments.

Center Village is completed with the opening of Copper One Lodge, The Mill Club, Tucker Mountain Lodge and Taylor's Crossing, including 250 lodging units and multiple shops, restaurants and bars.

2002

The opening of Passage Point marks the end of the Village at Copper development. Sling Shot Magic Carpet installed.

Intrawest joins the City of Denver in operating and upgrading the city-owned Winter Park Ski Area.

2003

West Lake is reopened with new shops, restaurants and bars.

In January 2003, the OHG women's program celebrated its 10th anniversary with 55 members.

March 15, 2003 the Copper Mountain OHG celebrated their 25th Anniversary.

2004

The Cirque opens offering Copper's first quarter-share platinum rated property.

The Summit County Board of Commissioners killed a proposal by Intrawest to add 1,155 residential units and more than 150,000 square feet of commercial space to the resorts base citing concerns about density, parking, and the size of proposed buildings in the village.

2006

On October 26, 2006 Intrawest was officially acquired by Fortress Group LLC.

New York private-equity firm Fortress Investment Group acquires Intrawest for $2.8 billion, using mostly debt, at an interest rate of about 6.4 percent.

OHG supervisor Joe Quarantillo initiates the "Gold Ski Award" to honor one of the OHG Guides who was nominated by the members for their focus on the members' experience during the season.

2007

Intrawest purchases Steamboat Ski Resort for $239.1 million from American Skiing Co., making Intrawest owner or manager of 11 North American ski resorts.

2008

Fortress injects $100 million into Intrawest on the day the company is due to pay or refinance $1.68 billion in debt.

Copper Mountain receives unanimous approval from the Summit County Board of County Commissioners for the next stage of village and base area development, which stands to add 590 units of density to the Resort while improving resort transportation and pedestrian flow, establishing ongoing funding for community programs, and construction of a multi-user recreation path throughout the resort base area.

2009

On December 18, 2009, the Powdr Corporation purchases Copper Mountain from Intrawest.

2010

On June 29, 2010, Copper Mountain notified the OHG organization and Volunteer Guides that the OHG program was being eliminated.

On July 18, 2010, the present OHG members filed legal papers to the State of Colorado to form Over the Hill Gang Summit, Inc.

On August 6, 2010, the Mountain and the OHG Advisory Team met to review the details and the program's future, addressing the Mountain's concerns and finding a path to continuing the program.

2012

Don Coleman, manager of the Adult Ski School at Copper Mountain works with a core team of guides and members to begin the revitalization of the Copper Mountain OHG.

Moe Mosley, the last living OHG Founder of the three retired from guiding and teaching skiing at Copper Mountain in the 2012/2013 ski season.

2017

As part of a $20M upgrade to the mountain and village, the new Kokomo Express high-speed quad chairlift was installed during the summer, together with the Rocky Mountain Coaster, the longest alpine coaster in North America, which operates in both summer and winter. Koko's lodge is built at the top of the new Kokomo Express providing food and warming, offering a pause after the quick ride up the lift, making the gentle beauty of the western part of the mountain more accessible and enjoyable for more people as they first explore the possibilities.

History of Snowfall

History of snow fall measurements in inches:

SKI SEASON	SNOWFALL IN INCHES	SKI SEASON	SNOWFALL IN INCHES
1972–1973	198	86–87	177
73–74	276	87–88	238
74–75	261	88–89	221
75–76	225	89–90	198
76–77	144	90–91	279
77–78	323	91–92	235
78–79	241	92–93	413
79–80	277	93–94	301
80–81	157	94–95	348
81–82	269	95–96	391
82–83	293	96–97	380
83–84	432	97–98	303
84–85	243	98–99	273
85–86	294	99–2000	301

SKI SEASON	SNOWFALL IN INCHES	SKI SEASON	SNOWFALL IN INCHES
2000–01	330	09–10	227
01–02	226	10–11	390
02–03	331	11–12	174
03–04	238	12–13	245
04–05	257	13–14	358
05–06	401	14–15	278
06–07	280	15–16	275
07–08	336	16–17	245
08–09	328		

Note: In 2003 the Mountain recorded snowfall near Solitude. Effective with the 2013–2014 season totals include October snowfall. Source: Copper Mountain PR Department.

Acknowledgements

The journey of writing and publishing a history of a movement cannot be completed in a vacuum. We are very thankful for the many friends and colleagues who helped us to compile and sift through copious amounts of research, information, data, and documents spanning 40 years of growth and the experiences of thousands of seniors across the country who were far from ready to tame their passion for snowsports upon reaching the ripe age of 50.

Much gratitude to Dr. Lance Secretan and his team at The Secretan Center Inc., Steve Hultquist and his loving family, both of whom have been great friends, and were an inspiration, along with the Moe-mentum team of quality administrative personnel who performed numerous hours of research and word processing of materials for this book.

Thanks to the following people who have contributed information to this wonderful program we call OHG. Please forgive any omissions. We salute and offer gratitude to:

Jay Abbott	Chuck Armstrong
Mark and Polly Addison	David Barry
Ray Allen	Floyd Bashant
Su Allen	Dennis and Sherri Beasley
Fred Ambler	Bob and Ann Beck
Glen Anderson	Sally Brand
Norm Anderson	Dodi Cariaso
Vino Anthony	Earl Clark

Chris Cocallas
Don Coleman
Lynda Collins
Chris Colman
Steve Combs
Andy Daly
Joel Day
Don Coleman
Lynda Collins
Chris Colman
Steve Combs
Andy Daly
Joel Day
Moe Dixon
Bill Douglas
Kirsti Eastman Anderson
Holly Emrick
Ken Emrick
Bill and Janis Erdkamp
Doug Erickson
Stew and Linda Everard
Mark "Sharky" Fish
Roger & Karen Foreman
Pete Franklin
Chuck Froelicher
Jim Galbreath
Neil and Kay Geitner
Mark Gidney
Jack & Sharon Godwin
Butch Graves
Dick Guyer

Tom Henderson
Rob Hill
Mike Homier
Rick Hopper
Jim Isham
Bob Jackson
Gene Jencsok
Stephan Jencsok
Ernie Jessen
Mary Jessen
Winnie Johnson
Jim Johnson
Dean Jones
Mark Jones
Mike Kelley
Tom Kilroy
Aleda Kresge
Paul Kresge
Mike Klysa
Nancy Lamphere
Larry Lash
Walt Laub
Bob Layton
Jim and Angie Leibold
Ron and Maggie Lemon
Chuck Levi
Chuck and Penny Lewis
Ed Lincoln
Jim and Marty Lincoln
Chuck Lisle
Governor Love

Bill Magill
Ray and Rosie May
Harry McNeil
Janice Moser
Harry Mosgrove
Janice Mulvaney
Dick Over
Joe Peterson
Gary Pogliano (Pog)
Joe Quarantillo
Gary Rodgers
Dave Sanctuary
Robbie Scholl
Bob Seibert
Sandy Shellworth Hildner
Bill ("Slot-car") Sloatman
Tom Snow
Pete and Joan Sowinski

Joe Stanski
Claudia Stein
Tom Stein
Tom Stein Jr.
Sara Swain
Cliff Taylor
Tammy Tharatt
Doug Trieste
Norma Tucker
Harley Van De Wege
Melinda Van Gundy
Jennifer Walker
David Wallerstein
Lee Wardman
Bill and Shirley Wegert
Carl Weller
Eames Yates
Ken Zimmerman

Thanks to the Administrative Team

Kim Jewell
Mia Tsuchimoto
Stacy McClure
Marissa Mills

Jennifer Herrera
Shannon Ratts
Kathleen Lynch
Tricia Field (Secretan Center)

The authors would especially like to thank those special souls behind the scenes—the trio's wives and cherished life partners of many years who have been instrumental and supportive of this venture during difficult times as the authors brought this book to life:

Tricia Secretan (we lost Tricia on 9/10/2014, a wonderful life partner who gave unwavering support to this venture) and Terry Hultquist and Lou Guy Mosley.

Thanks to the Members and Guides

After the basic foundation, business structure, and programs were in place for the Over the Hill Gang, it took hundreds of volunteers with a vision, commitment, foresight, and assistance to bring these organizations to the level they enjoy today. We thank all who contributed to this amazing program over the years and who will do so into the future.

The success of these three senior ski organizations in Colorado, the Over the Hill Gang (OHG), OHG International, and SkiMeisters, is due to the guides, the membership, and the mountains that continue to draw them into the alpine adventure.

The three founders were in the right place at the right time, and considered themselves to be very fortunate to have been surrounded by so many wonderful people who joined them to assist with these programs.

Since this senior ski adventure started at Copper Mountain, we are very grateful to have had the support of Copper's management team throughout the years, including Copper's leaders, chief executives Chuck Lewis, Andy Daly, Harry Mosgrove, David Barry, and Gary Rodgers.

Special acknowledgment goes to the Copper Mountain Ski School directors and the Adult Ski School supervisors who played such a formative role during the earliest years. Their support helped to carry this program through some unusual and challenging situations.

From the very beginning of Copper Mountain's Over the Hill Gang (OHG), the entire mountain staff, and later, the staff of the OHG International and SkiMeisters, have continued to grow in their enthusiasm and commitment, generating members' unwavering pride in their organizations. Many of these members have belonged to all three organizations at one time or another.

Moe Mosley on behalf of the Founders

Thanks to the SkiMeisters

We would like to thank the following people who assisted with information on the SkiMeisters Section of the OHG Book:

Dee Irwin	Dick Over
Ron Lemon	Arthur Shenkin
Rosie May	Shirley Wegert
Janice Mulvany	Dick Williams
Fred Nyland	

For more information, see the SkiMeisters website at *http://www.skimeisters.org.*